W9-CCS-308

SUPER FOOD
Family classics

JAMIE OLIVER

HarperCollins*Publishers*Ltd

ALSO BY JAMIE OLIVER

FOOD PHOTOGRAPHY
Jamie Oliver

PORTRAIT PHOTOGRAPHY
Paul Stuart

DESIGN
Superfantastic
wearesuperfantastic.com

To my lovely wife, Jools,

who somehow holds the growing Oliver family together,
even though it's crazy—most of the time!

CONTENTS

EASY, SUPER-TASTY,
& PACKED WITH GOODNESS

That's what you guys told me you wanted from the recipes in a healthy family cookbook, and that's exactly what I've delivered throughout these pages. I've basically taken a whole host of classic comfort food dishes and ultimate family favorites that I know you love, and cooked, rewritten, tested, and edited them to make sure they fit bang into my super-food philosophy. What does that mean? Well, it guarantees that not only will you be eating exciting meals that will tickle your taste buds, are super-delicious, and will fill you up, but every one of those meals is totally balanced and will help to fuel, revive, restore, and energize you, too.

The word "family" means something different to us all, especially when it comes to food. For me, it's about food that's cozy, comforting, and made for sharing, and all too often that can mean food that's not so good for you, too. Not in this book! This is all about encouraging you to enjoy great food that nourishes you every day, whether you're tucking in on your own, with family, or with friends. I've got loads of inspiration on the breakfast front with tasty ideas that all come in under 400 calories, as well as a bonus chapter of Kitchen Hacks—these are elements you can make in advance and have up your sleeve, ready to kick off meals with ease. All the other chapters—from Quick Fixes to Pasta & Risotto, Traybakes to Curries & Stews—will have you totally covered when it comes to lunch and dinner. These recipes all fit into a framework of 600 calories or less, so just mix up your choices among the chapters and across the week, and you'll be in a good place (see page 244). If you can cook food like this three or four days of the week, it will only have a positive impact on your, and your family's, health. You'll find nutritional info on every recipe page, should you wish to read it, and for all those lunch and dinner meals I've made sure you'll be getting at least two portions of veg and fruit per plate. Every recipe is designed to give you a brilliant boost of goodness.

Just like in *Everyday Super Food*, I've taken all the food photos, because that allowed me to be super-close to the recipes, interrogating and honing the ingredients, methods, and techniques to be the absolute best they can. Backed up by a bumper section of health and well-being info at the back of the book, I want *Super Food Family Classics* to arm you with everything you and your family need to be the best *you* can be, and to live healthier, happier lives.

BREAKFAST

Kick off your day the right way, fueling
your body to be the best it can be

CHOCOLATE PORRIDGE
GREEK YOGURT & FRESH SEASONAL FRUIT

___ Quality cocoa powder creates a luxurious feeling of comforting chocolaty goodness here, but ___
without all the sugar and saturated fat we'd get from actually adding chocolate to the mix

MAKES 12 PORTIONS
20 MINUTES

7 oz blanched hazelnuts

7 oz Medjool dates

4 cups rolled oats

2 teaspoons vanilla extract

3 heaping tablespoons quality
cocoa powder

1 orange

FOR EACH PORTION

¾ cup + 5 teaspoons coconut
water

1 heaping tablespoon Greek
yogurt

3 oz fresh fruit, such as
raspberries, blackberries, sliced
banana, grated apple and pear,
segments of orange

optional: 1 pinch of ground
cinnamon or quality
cocoa powder

Toast the hazelnuts in a dry pan on a medium heat until golden, tossing often, then tip into a food processor. Tear the pits out of the dates and add the flesh to the processor with half the oats, the vanilla extract, and cocoa powder. Finely grate in the orange zest and pulse until fine, then stir the mixture back through the rest of the oats. Pour into an airtight jar, ready to use.

When you want a portion, simply put 2 oz of the mixture into a saucepan with the coconut water and heat gently over a medium-low heat for 3 minutes, or until it's the consistency that you like, stirring regularly and adding splashes of water to loosen, if needed. Serve each portion with a spoonful of Greek yogurt and 3 oz of fresh fruit. It's also nice finished with a pinch of cinnamon or a dusting of cocoa, if you like. And remember, if you up the number of portions you're cooking at one time, simply adjust the cooking time accordingly. Chocolate porridge—how cool is that!

Get ahead & batch it up

Make up a batch of this dry porridge mixture and it'll keep happily
for up to 2 weeks, making your brekkie routine super-easy.

CALORIES	FAT	SAT FAT	PROTEIN	CARBS	SUGAR	SALT	FIBER	1 PORTION VEG & FRUIT
356kcal	15.9g	2.9g	11.3g	45.2g	21.2g	0.2g	6.3g	

BRILLIANT BOILED EGGS
4 DELICIOUS & BALANCED WAYS

Eating eggs is a super-easy way to boost our nutrient intake—they contain high-quality protein, and a nice wide range of essential vitamins, minerals, and trace elements

ALL SERVE 1

BRITISH STYLE

Rinse and soft-boil **1 large egg** in a pan of bubbling water on a medium-high heat for 5½ minutes, also blanching **5 oz of trimmed large asparagus spears.** Meanwhile, toast **1 slice of whole-grain bread (1¾ oz)** and cut into soldiers. Drain the asparagus, toss with **1 teaspoon of light cream cheese,** then pile onto the toast and finely grate over the tiniest amount of **Parmesan cheese.** Slice the top off the egg and tuck in.

INDIAN STYLE

Soft-boil **1 large egg** in a pan of bubbling water on a medium-high heat for 5½ minutes. Meanwhile, spread **1 teaspoon of jalfrezi curry paste** over **1 whole-wheat chapatti,** sprinkle with **1 pinch of raw sesame seeds,** and toast in a dry frying pan on both sides, then cut into triangles. Wash and halve **3 oz of small heirloom carrots,** and dress with a squeeze of **lemon juice.** Serve with **1 tablespoon of plain yogurt** swirled with **hot chili sauce.** Slice the top off the egg and tuck in.

MEXICAN STYLE

Soft-boil **1 large egg** in a pan of bubbling water on a medium-high heat for 5½ minutes. Meanwhile, dice **¼ of a ripe avocado** and **2½ oz of ripe cherry tomatoes,** and dress with a squeeze of **lime juice** and a few **fresh cilantro leaves.** Toast **1 corn tortilla,** cut into triangles, and sprinkle over the veg with **1 heaping teaspoon of cottage cheese** and a drizzle of **hot chili sauce.** Slice the top off the egg and tuck in.

SPANISH STYLE

Soft-boil **1 large egg** in a pan of bubbling water on a medium-high heat for 5½ minutes. Meanwhile, toast **1 slice of whole-grain bread (1¾ oz)** and lightly rub one side with the cut side of **½ a clove of garlic.** Squash in **3 halved ripe cherry tomatoes,** sprinkle with **1 pinch of dried oregano,** finely grate over **¼ oz of Manchego cheese,** and toast cheese-side down in a dry frying pan. Char **1 large peeled roasted red pepper** alongside it. Slice the top off the egg and tuck in.

CALORIES	FAT	SAT FAT	PROTEIN	CARBS	SUGAR	SALT	FIBER	1 PORTION VEG & FRUIT
269kcal	11.9g	3.6g	14.7g	25.5g	5.4g	1.1g	4.4g	

THESE VALUES ARE AN AVERAGE OF THE FOUR RECIPES ABOVE

BREAKFAST DOUGHNUTS
HONEY, JAMMY BLUEBERRIES, & YOGURT

— Beautiful blueberries add a vibrant pop of color to these tasty homemade doughnuts, while also giving us a vitamin C boost, helping us absorb the iron found in both flours —

SERVES 4

35 MINUTES

3¼ oz Medjool dates

heaping ¾ cup whole-grain self-rising flour

heaping ¾ cup self-rising flour, plus extra for dusting

1 oz ground almonds

1 large egg

olive oil

11 oz blueberries

1 tablespoon liquid honey

4 tablespoons Greek yogurt

optional: ground cinnamon

Tear the pits out of the dates and place the flesh in a food processor with the flours, ground almonds, egg, a tiny pinch of sea salt, and ¼ cup of water. Blitz until combined and forming a ball of dough, then roughly knead on a clean flour-dusted surface for just 2 minutes. Roll out the dough ¾ inch thick, then use an 3-inch cutter (or a pint glass) to cut out two rounds. Use a 1¼-inch cutter (or the end of a paper towel roll!) to cut a hole in the center of each one, then use those center bits and the remaining cut-offs of dough and roll it out again, repeating the process until you have four doughnuts in total.

Simmer the doughnuts in a large pan of gently boiling water for 5 minutes, very carefully turning them over halfway through. Place a large frying pan on a medium heat with 1 tablespoon of oil. Drain the doughnuts well, then carefully transfer them to the frying pan to get golden for 10 minutes, turning regularly to build up a nice crust. Once looking good, add the blueberries to the pan, then drizzle over the honey. Jiggle and shake the pan over the heat for a couple of minutes, using a spoon to keep turning the doughnuts in all that lovely jammy blueberry juice. When it looks nice and shiny and the doughnuts are purple, ripple the yogurt through the pan and divide between your plates. Nice with a sprinkling of cinnamon, to finish.

- *Kitchen hack* -

If you can't find whole-grain self-rising flour, you can add 2 teaspoons of baking powder per 1 cup of regular whole-wheat flour and sift well.

CALORIES	FAT	SAT FAT	PROTEIN	CARBS	SUGAR	SALT	FIBER	1 PORTION VEG & FRUIT
361kcal	11.3g	2.3g	12.5g	55.6g	21.4g	0.4g	4.8g	

TOASTED POPEYE BREAD
EGGS, VINE TOMATOES, & CHILI SAUCE

— Spinach is a brilliant ingredient to embrace at breakfast time—it's super-high in vitamin K, —
which we need to keep our bones strong and healthy. Popeye knew what he was doing!

SERVES 2

25 MINUTES

5½ oz ripe cherry tomatoes,
  on the vine

4 thin slices of whole-grain bread
  (1⅓ oz each)

3 large eggs

1 x ½ oz slice of smoked ham

3 oz baby spinach

2 tablespoons reduced-fat (2%)
  milk

1 heaping tablespoon cottage
  cheese

extra virgin olive oil

hot chili sauce

Preheat the grill to high. Lay the tomato vines in a large baking pan, prick each tomato with the tip of a sharp knife, and grill for 4 minutes, then add the bread to the pan to toast on both sides. Meanwhile, crack 1 egg into a blender, add the ham, spinach, a good pinch of black pepper, and the milk and blitz until smooth. Take the pan from under the grill and divide the green eggy mixture between the four pieces of toast, spreading it right out to the edges. Divide and dot over the cottage cheese, then pop back under the grill for another 4 minutes, or until starting to brown at the edges.

Meanwhile, dry fry the remaining 2 eggs in a non-stick frying pan on a medium heat, covering the pan with a lid to steam and coddle the eggs on the top—cook to your liking. Divide up the Popeye bread and serve each portion with an egg and half the grilled tomatoes. I like to finish with just a few drips of good oil, and a drizzle of chili sauce for a bit of a kick. Crush the tomatoes, tear up the bread, bust up the egg yolk, and devour.

CALORIES	FAT	SAT FAT	PROTEIN	CARBS	SUGAR	SALT	FIBER	1 PORTION VEG & FRUIT
356kcal	14.6g	4g	23.6g	31.8g	6.4g	1.4g	6.4g	

HEALTHY BALANCED BREAKFAST SMOOTHIES
4 SUPER-EXCITING & SATISFYING COMBOS

These tasty smoothies give us a total balanced brekkie, all in one nice, big glass. Each combo guarantees we're getting a portion of fruit or veg, plus some fiber from the whole grains

ALL SERVE 1

SUPER PURPLE

Squeeze the juice from **1 orange** into a blender, add ½ a ripe pear, 3 oz of fresh or frozen blackberries, ¼ cup of rolled oats, 1 scant cup of almond milk, 1 tablespoon of sunflower seeds, 1 pinch of fennel seeds, and 1 handful of ice cubes. Blitz until smooth, loosening with splashes of water until you get the perfect drinkable consistency. Pour into a big glass or decant into a bottle and enjoy.

SUPER CHOC

Peel and pit ½ **a ripe avocado** and place in a blender with **¼ cup of rolled oats, 6 tablespoons of reduced-fat (2%) milk, 1 oz of Medjool dates** (pitted), **1 heaping teaspoon each of quality cocoa powder and ground almonds**, and 1 handful of ice cubes. Blitz until smooth, loosening with splashes of water until you get the perfect drinkable consistency. Pour into a big glass or decant into a bottle and enjoy.

SUPER CREAMY

Peel **1 ripe banana** and place in a blender with **1 slice of soft brown bread (1¾ oz), 6 tablespoons of reduced-fat (2%) milk, 1 heaping teaspoon of peanut butter, ½ a teaspoon of ground cinnamon**, and 1 handful of ice cubes. Blitz until smooth, loosening with splashes of water until you get the perfect drinkable consistency. Pour into a big glass or decant into a bottle and enjoy. Nice with an extra pinch of cinnamon, to finish.

SUPER GREEN

Peel ½ **a ripe banana** and place in a blender with **½ an apple, 1½ oz of baby spinach, ¼ cup of rolled oats, ⅔ cup of reduced-fat (2%) milk, 1 tablespoon of almond butter** (or you can swap in your favorite nut butter), and 1 handful of ice cubes. Blitz until smooth, loosening with splashes of water until you get the perfect drinkable consistency. Pour into a big glass or decant into a bottle and enjoy.

CALORIES	FAT	SAT FAT	PROTEIN	CARBS	SUGAR	SALT	FIBER	1 PORTION VEG & FRUIT
325kcal	12.5g	2.7g	11.4g	43.9g	21.8g	0.3g	5.4g	

THESE VALUES ARE AN AVERAGE OF THE FOUR RECIPES ABOVE

STRAWBERRY BUCKWHEAT PANCAKES
GREEK YOGURT & ROSEMARY MAPLE SYRUP

— This super-tasty pancake batter is perfect for vegans, plus buckwheat flour contains the mineral manganese, which we need to keep all our connective tissue strong and healthy —

SERVES 4
30 MINUTES

1¼ cups almond milk

1 teaspoon vanilla extract

2½ oz blanched almonds

heaping ¾ cup buckwheat flour

heaping ¾ cup rice flour

2 level teaspoons baking powder

1 ripe banana

olive oil

12 oz seasonal berries, such as
  strawberries, blackberries,
  raspberries, blueberries

1 sprig of fresh rosemary

maple syrup

4 tablespoons Greek yogurt

Pour the milk into a blender with the vanilla extract, almonds, flours, and baking powder. Peel and add the banana, then blitz until smooth. Place a large non-stick frying pan on a medium heat. Once hot, for each portion of two pancakes add 1 teaspoon of oil to the pan with 3 tablespoons of batter per pancake. Push some sliced strawberries or whole berries into the batter, then cook for 4 minutes, or until nicely golden on the bottom (the first pancakes are always slightly awkward as you're adjusting your temperature control). Flip over, apply a little pressure with a slotted spatula, and cook for 2 minutes, or until golden on the other side, then transfer to a plate, fruit-side up. Wipe out the pan with a ball of paper towel and repeat the process.

Stick the sprig of rosemary into the maple syrup bottle and use it to lightly brush syrup over the hot pancakes. Top each portion with a dollop of yogurt and serve with extra berries on the side.

Get ahead

This batter will sit happily in the fridge, so make it the day before, or, if you're cooking for fewer than four, simply make up the whole batch to do you for a couple of days.

CALORIES	FAT	SAT FAT	PROTEIN	CARBS	SUGAR	SALT	FIBER	1 PORTION
398kcal	15.7g	2.4g	12.3g	53.9g	15.9g	0.7g	3.5g	VEG & FRUIT

MAGIC POACHED EGGS
2 WAYS

Brilliant, bright egg yolks are high in vitamin D, something we lack in the winter months
when we're less exposed to sunlight, and which our muscles need to function properly

EACH SERVES 1

TRUFFLED MUSHROOM

Lay a 16-inch sheet of non-PVC plastic wrap flat on a work surface and rub with a little **truffle oil**. Finely slice
1 chestnut or cremini mushroom and arrange in the center of the sheet, then carefully crack **1 large egg** on top.
Pull in the sides of the plastic wrap and—very important—gently squeeze out any air around the egg. Twist, then
tie a knot in the plastic wrap to secure the egg snugly inside. Poach the parcel in a pan of simmering water for 6 to
7 minutes for soft-poached, or until cooked to your liking. Place a colander or bamboo steamer above the pan and
wilt **3 oz of spinach** as the egg poaches. Meanwhile, toast **1 thick slice of whole-grain bread with seeds (1¾ oz)**
and spread **1 heaping teaspoon of cream cheese** on it like butter. Squeeze any excess liquid out of the spinach, then
spoon over the toast. Snip open the plastic wrap parcel, unwrap the egg, place proudly on top, season, and tuck in.

HERBY SMOKED SALMON

Lay a 16-inch sheet of non-PVC plastic wrap flat on a work surface and rub with a little **extra virgin olive oil**.
Finely chop some **fresh chives** and sprinkle in the center of the sheet, then slice and lay over **⅓ oz of smoked
salmon** and carefully crack **1 large egg** on top. Pull in the sides of the plastic wrap and—very important—gently
squeeze out any air around the egg. Twist, then tie a knot in the plastic wrap to secure the egg snugly inside. Poach
the parcel in a pan of simmering water for 6 to 7 minutes for soft-poached, or until cooked to your liking. Place a
colander or bamboo steamer above the pan and wilt **3 oz of spinach** as the egg poaches. Meanwhile, toast **1 thick
slice of whole-grain bread with seeds (1¾ oz)** and spread **1 heaping teaspoon of cream cheese** on it like butter.
Squeeze any excess liquid out of the spinach, then spoon over the toast. Snip open the plastic wrap parcel, unwrap
the egg, and place proudly on top. Serve with **a wedge of lemon** for squeezing over, then season and tuck in.

CALORIES	FAT	SAT FAT	PROTEIN	CARBS	SUGAR	SALT	FIBER	1 PORTION
272kcal	13.5g	4g	16.5g	20.5g	2.7g	1.2g	5g	VEG & FRUIT

THESE VALUES ARE AN AVERAGE OF THE TWO RECIPES ABOVE

PINEAPPLE PANCAKE MESS
YOGURT, COCONUT, CASHEWS, & LIME

Juicy, super-ripe, sweet pineapple is a great source of the mineral manganese, which is one of the nutrients our bodies need in order to keep our metabolic systems nice and healthy

SERVES 4

35 MINUTES

1½ oz unsalted cashew nuts

2 tablespoons unsweetened desiccated coconut flakes

1 ripe pineapple

4 cardamom pods

1 cup all-purpose whole-wheat flour

1¼ cups reduced-fat (2%) milk

1 large egg

1 teaspoon vanilla extract

1 pinch of ground cinnamon

olive oil

4 tablespoons plain yogurt

1 lime

optional: manuka honey

Toast the cashews in a large non-stick frying pan on a medium heat until lightly golden, add the coconut for just 30 seconds, then tip both into a pestle and mortar and lightly crush. Trim the ends off the pineapple, cut off the skin, quarter it lengthways, and cut away the core. Chop the flesh into ½-inch slices. Return the dry pan to a medium-high heat and cook the pineapple for 5 to 10 minutes, or until caramelized, tossing regularly, then remove to a warm plate.

Meanwhile, crush the cardamom pods, putting just the inner seeds into a blender with the flour, milk, egg, vanilla extract, cinnamon, and a tiny pinch of sea salt. Blitz until smooth. Drizzle a little oil into the empty pineapple pan, then carefully wipe it around and out with a ball of paper towel. Add just enough batter to lightly cover the base of the pan, cook until golden on both sides, then remove to a second plate. Repeat the process, stacking up the pancakes as you go and covering with a kitchen towel to keep warm.

Either make up individual portions, or do a sharing platter for the middle of the table. Randomly tear, fold, and layer up the pancakes with the caramelized pineapple, spoonfuls of yogurt and sprinklings of crushed cashews and coconut. Repeat until you've used up all the ingredients, then finely grate over the lime zest. Nice served with a drizzle of honey, if you fancy.

CALORIES	FAT	SAT FAT	PROTEIN	CARBS	SUGAR	SALT	FIBER	1 PORTION VEG & FRUIT
309kcal	10.9g	3.9g	12.5g	43.4g	18.8g	0.3g	3.7g	

ENGLISH BREAKFAST FRITTATA
BACON, MUSHROOMS, SPUDS, & TOMATOES

Eggs act as the binder to bring together all our favorite brekkie ingredients here, plus they're super-high in protein, which we need for growth and repair, so this is a great post-gym go-to

SERVES 4

35 MINUTES

8 oz baby chestnut or cremini mushrooms

4 ripe mixed-color medium tomatoes

2 slices of whole-grain bread (1¾ oz each)

7 oz potatoes

2 rashers of smoked bacon

2 sprigs of fresh rosemary

olive oil

3 oz baby spinach

6 large eggs

⅓ oz Parmesan cheese

Preheat the broiler to high. Wipe the mushrooms clean and chop in half. Halve the tomatoes. Arrange the mushrooms and tomatoes cut-side up in a pan and broil for 6 to 8 minutes, to get nice and golden on that side only—keep an eye on them (dry broiling mushrooms really brings out their incredible nutty flavor). Toast the bread alongside until golden, then remove it all.

Meanwhile, coarsely grate the potatoes in nice long strokes and sprinkle with a pinch of sea salt to help draw out any excess liquid. Finely chop the bacon and pick the rosemary leaves. Place a 10½-inch non-stick ovenproof frying pan on a medium heat with 2 teaspoons of oil. Fry the bacon and rosemary leaves for 2 minutes, or until golden. Squeeze any excess liquid out of the grated potato, stir into the pan, and cook for 5 minutes, or until golden, stirring regularly.

Pile the spinach into the pan and tear in the toast in chunks, then add the mushrooms and tomatoes. Use tongs to gently toss and mix it all together until the spinach has wilted. Meanwhile, in a large bowl, beat the eggs with the finely grated Parmesan and a pinch of black pepper. Once the spinach has wilted, pour the contents of the pan into the bowl of eggs and gently fold together. Pour back into the pan, then transfer to the broiler for 5 minutes, or until cooked to your liking. Slide onto a board, cut into wedges, and serve.

CALORIES	FAT	SAT FAT	PROTEIN	CARBS	SUGAR	SALT	FIBER	2 PORTIONS VEG & FRUIT
291kcal	14.8g	4g	18.6g	21.3g	3.9g	1.4g	4.1g	

ROASTED STONE FRUIT
COCONUT, DATE, & OAT CRUMBLE

Two of our crumble ingredients here—mighty oats and beautifully sweet dates—are super-high in fiber, helping to keep our guts healthy and happy, and keeping us regular!

MAKES 12 PORTIONS
55 MINUTES

6 oranges

1 tablespoon balsamic vinegar

1 vanilla bean

5 oz ripe strawberries

7 oz Medjool dates

2½ cups rolled oats

¾ cup unsweetened desiccated
  coconut flakes

extra virgin olive oil

4½ lbs mixed seasonal stone fruit,
  such as plums, peaches,
  apricots, cherries

PER PORTION

1 tablespoon plain yogurt

Preheat the oven to 400°F. Halve the oranges and squeeze all the juice into a large roasting dish with the balsamic. Halve the vanilla bean lengthways and scrape out the seeds, then add both bean and seeds to the dish. Grate in the strawberries, mix together, and pop into the oven to warm through while you prep your crumble and fruit.

For the crumble, tear the pits out of the dates and place the flesh in a food processor with the oats, coconut flakes, 1 tablespoon of oil, and ½ cup of water, then blitz into a crumble. Pour into a roasting pan or dish (16 x 12 inches) and spread out into an even layer. Wash all the fruit, then halve or quarter, removing the stones as you go. Pull the dish of warm, delicious juices out of the oven and gently stir in all the fruit. Return to the top rack of the oven, place the crumble on the rack underneath, and cook for 45 minutes, or until the fruit is soft and sticky and the crumble is nicely golden. Stir the crumble occasionally as it cooks to break it up and give it a nice even color.

Serve up however many portions you want while it's all warm, adding 1 tablespoon of yogurt to each one. Once cool, decant the rest of the crumble portions into an airtight jar to enjoy in the days that follow, and pop the fruit into the fridge, where it will keep happily for up to 5 days.

CALORIES	FAT	SAT FAT	PROTEIN	CARBS	SUGAR	SALT	FIBER	2 PORTIONS
218kcal	5.6g	2.6g	4.8g	37.2g	22.8g	0g	3.6g	VEG & FRUIT

CRISPY RICE PANCAKES
CURRIED CHICKPEAS, EGGS, & COCONUT SALSA

Comforting chickpeas add great taste and texture in this brekkie, plus they're high in folic acid, a B vitamin we need for psychological function, basically allowing us to think properly!

SERVES 4

30 MINUTES

⅛ x ¼-oz package of yeast

¾ cup rice flour

olive oil

1 heaping teaspoon jalfrezi curry paste (see page 236)

½–1 fresh red chile

1 bunch of scallions

½ x 19-oz can of chickpeas

3½ oz baby spinach

1½-inch piece of fresh gingerroot

2 ripe tomatoes

1 lime

2 tablespoons unsweetened desiccated coconut flakes

½ a bunch of fresh cilantro (½ oz)

4 large eggs

4 heaping tablespoons plain yogurt

In a bowl, whisk the yeast into 1 cup of lukewarm water, then gradually whisk in the flour and a pinch of sea salt until smooth. Put aside. Place a frying pan on a medium heat with 1 teaspoon of oil and the curry paste. Finely slice half the chile and just the top green halves of the scallions and add to the pan. Cook and stir for 5 minutes, then add the chickpeas (juice and all), and the spinach. Bring to a boil, then simmer on a low heat until needed.

To make the salsa, trim and finely slice the whites of the scallions, along with the remaining chile, and place in a bowl. Peel and finely grate in the ginger. Quarter and seed the tomatoes, then finely dice and add the flesh to the bowl. Finely grate over the lime zest, squeeze in the juice, add the coconut and cilantro leaves, and mix well, then taste and season to perfection.

For the pancakes, place a small non-stick frying pan on a medium heat, drizzle with a little oil, then carefully wipe it around and out with a ball of paper towel. Stirring your batter well each time, add a quarter to the pan, swiftly swirling it around and up the sides to create extra crispy bits. Cook for about 5 minutes on the underside only, until dark golden—have faith—and when it's colored, use a spatula to ease it away from the sides and slide it out. Repeat with the remaining batter, and just before you start the last pancake, poach the eggs to your liking in a large pan of simmering water.

Serve each pancake with a spoonful of curried chickpeas and coconut salsa, a dollop of yogurt, and with a poached egg sitting proudly on top.

CALORIES	FAT	SAT FAT	PROTEIN	CARBS	SUGAR	SALT	FIBER	1 PORTION VEG & FRUIT
319kcal	11.4g	3.8g	15.8g	38.4g	4.7g	0.9g	4.9g	

MANGO LASSI BIRCHER
GINGER, NUTS, TURMERIC, & FENNEL SEEDS

—— Packed with all sorts of goodness, oats contain beta-glucans, a type of fiber that helps to keep our cholesterol levels in check, in turn helping to protect us against heart disease ——

SERVES 4

20 MINUTES
PLUS SOAKING

4 cardamom pods

¼ cup flaxseeds

½ teaspoon ground turmeric

¼ teaspoon ground cinnamon

¾-inch piece of fresh gingerroot

1 heaping tablespoon peanut
    butter

2 cups rolled oats

1¼ cups reduced-fat (2%) milk

2 tablespoons plain yogurt

1 lime

1 small ripe banana

10 oz frozen mango

1 tablespoon unsweetened
    desiccated coconut

¾ oz shelled unsalted pistachios

½ teaspoon fennel seeds

Crush the cardamom pods, putting just the inner seeds in a food processor with the flaxseeds, 1 pinch of the turmeric, the cinnamon, peeled ginger, peanut butter, and half the oats, then pulse until fine. Add the milk, yogurt, and lime juice, peel and tear in the banana, then add the frozen mango and blitz until well combined. Decant into a bowl, stir in the remaining oats and the coconut, then cover and place in the fridge to soak overnight.

To make the crunchy sprinkle, toast the pistachios and fennel seeds for 1 minute in a non-stick frying pan on a medium heat. Turn the heat off and, once cool, lightly crush with the end of a rolling pin, mixing in the remaining turmeric. Remove however many portions of Bircher you want to serve up, and loosen to your desired consistency with a little extra milk, if needed. Divide between your bowls, sprinkle some pistachio crunch in the center, and tuck in. Any leftovers will keep happily in the fridge for up to 2 days.

CALORIES	FAT	SAT FAT	PROTEIN	CARBS	SUGAR	SALT	FIBER	1 PORTION
399kcal	15.7g	3.9g	13.4g	49.4g	15.2g	0.2g	10.5g	VEG & FRUIT

AVOCADO ON RYE TOAST
LOADS OF INSPIRATION - PART 1

I'm told that in the UK avocados are now more popular than oranges! This breakfast favorite is a source of vitamin E, which acts as an antioxidant, helping to protect our cells

EACH COMBO SERVES 1

Spread **1 heaping teaspoon of light cream cheese** over **1 x 2½-oz slice of rye bread or toast,** then sprinkle over **1 teaspoon of mixed seeds.** Cut **½ a ripe avocado** into thin wedges and arrange on top, squeeze over a little **lemon juice**, season to taste, and drizzle with **1 teaspoon of extra virgin olive oil**, then finely slice and scatter over ½ **a fresh red chile,** to taste.

Spread **1 heaping teaspoon of ricotta cheese** over **1 x 2½-oz slice of rye bread or toast.** Finely slice **½ a ripe avocado** and **1 ripe tomato** and toss with a squeeze of **lemon juice,** then season to taste and arrange on the toast. Sprinkle with **1 teaspoon of toasted pine nuts** and **a few fresh baby basil leaves,** if you've got them.

Use a fork to smash up **½ a ripe avocado, ½ a ripe peeled banana, 1 heaping teaspoon of light cream cheese,** and **1 teaspoon of peanut butter** until smooth. Spread over **1 x 2½-oz slice of rye bread or toast,** sprinkle over **1 teaspoon of toasted sesame seeds,** and finish with the seeds from ¼ **of a pomegranate,** piled on top.

Spread **1 heaping teaspoon of light cream cheese** over **1 x 2½-oz slice of rye bread or toast.** Wilt **1 large handful of spinach or seasonal greens,** toss with a squeeze of **lemon juice,** season to taste, and pile on top. Add **½ a soft-boiled egg, ½ a sliced ripe avocado,** a few **fresh cilantro leaves,** and **1 pinch of curry powder,** to finish.

In a bowl, use a fork to smash up **1 cooked beet** with **1 teaspoon of hummus** and **1 teaspoon of cottage cheese**, then season to taste and spread over **1 x 2½-oz slice of rye bread or toast**. Place **½ a ripe avocado** on top, drizzle with **1 teaspoon of extra virgin olive oil**, and sprinkle with **1 teaspoon of mixed seeds**.

Quickly cook **1 tablespoon of frozen baby peas**, then drain and use a fork to smash them up with **½ a ripe avocado**, **1 heaping teaspoon of cottage cheese**, a squeeze of **lemon juice**, and a few finely chopped **fresh mint leaves**, if you have them. Season to taste and spread over **1 x 2½-oz slice of rye bread or toast**, then drizzle with **1 teaspoon of extra virgin olive oil** and scatter over **1 teaspoon of crushed almonds**.

Heat **½ x 15-oz can of drained black beans** in a frying pan on a medium heat with **1 teaspoon of chipotle Tabasco sauce** for 5 minutes, then stir through **1 heaping teaspoon of cottage cheese** and pour onto **1 x 2½-oz slice of rye bread or toast**. Chop up **½ a ripe avocado** and **½ a fresh red chile**, toss with a squeeze of **lime juice**, and pile on top with a few **fresh cilantro leaves**.

Fork up, smash, and spread **½ a ripe avocado** over **1 x 2½-oz slice of rye bread or toast**. Slice and add **½ a ripe beefsteak tomato**, pit and tear over **2 black olives**, and crumble over **¼ oz of feta cheese**. Finish with **1 pinch of dried oregano**, **1 teaspoon of extra virgin olive oil**, and a pinch of black pepper.

Spread **1 teaspoon of Marmite** and **1 heaping teaspoon of cottage cheese** over **1 x 2½ oz slice of rye bread or toast**. Peel and slice **½ a ripe avocado** and char in a dry frying pan with **4 trimmed chestnut or cremini mushrooms**, then pile on top. Chop and sprinkle over **2 ripe cherry tomatoes**, drizzle with **1 teaspoon of extra virgin olive oil**, then add a squeeze of **lemon juice** and a pinch of black pepper.

AVOCADO ON RYE TOAST
LOADS OF INSPIRATION – PART 2

— Rye bread is really widely available now—that's great news, as it's high in chloride, which
we need to make hydrochloric acid in our stomachs so we can digest our food properly —

EACH COMBO SERVES 1

Fork up, smash, and spread ½ **a ripe avocado** over **1 x 2½-oz slice of rye bread
or toast.** Toss **1 small handful of arugula** with a squeeze of **lemon juice**, pile it in
the center of **1 slice of prosciutto**, then wrap it up and place on top. Chop and add
2 ripe cherry tomatoes, then shave over **¼ oz of Parmesan cheese** and sprinkle
with a pinch of black pepper, to finish.

Fork up, smash, and spread ½ **a ripe avocado** and **1 heaping teaspoon of ricotta
cheese** over **1 x 2½-oz slice of rye bread or toast.** Blanch **3 oz of broccolini**,
drain, toss with a squeeze of **lemon juice** and **1 teaspoon of extra virgin olive oil**,
then season to taste. Pile on top, and sprinkle with **1 teaspoon of crushed toasted
hazelnuts** and **1 pinch of dried red chili flakes**.

Spread **1 heaping teaspoon of light cream cheese** over **1 x 2½-oz slice of rye bread
or toast.** Trim and char **4 scallions** in a dry frying pan, then chop up with ½ **a large
roasted peeled red pepper**, ½ **a ripe avocado**, and **1 sprig of fresh Italian parsley**.
Toss with **1 teaspoon of extra virgin olive oil** and a squeeze of **lemon juice**, then
season to taste, and pile on top with **1 teaspoon of halved almonds**.

Use a fork to smash up ½ **a ripe avocado**, ½ **a ripe banana**, **1 heaping teaspoon of
light cream cheese**, and **1 teaspoon of quality cocoa powder** until smooth. Spread
over **1 x 2½-oz slice of rye bread or toast**, dot over a few **raspberries** and **2 teaspoons
of toasted hazelnuts**, then shave over a tiny bit of **dark chocolate (70%)**, if you like.

Slice ½ **a ripe avocado** and arrange over **1 x 2½-oz slice of rye bread or toast**, then squeeze over a little **lemon juice**. Finely slice and add a few rounds of **cucumber** and some chopped **fresh chives**, lay over **¾ oz of smoked salmon** in waves, then finish with **1 heaping teaspoon of cottage cheese** and a pinch of black pepper.

Purée ½ **a ripe avocado** with a squeeze of **lemon juice**, season to taste, and spread over **1 x 2½-oz slice of rye bread or toast**. Char **1 corn on the cob** on a dry grill pan, slice off the kernels, and pile on top. Dollop over **1 heaping teaspoon of cottage cheese** and drizzle with **1 teaspoon of extra virgin olive oil** and a little **hot chili sauce**.

Spread **1 heaping teaspoon of light cream cheese** over **1 x 2½-oz slice of rye bread or toast**. Slice ½ **a ripe avocado** and arrange on top. Loosen **1 teaspoon of English mustard** with a squeeze of **lemon juice**, and spread it onto **1 oz of hot smoked trout**. Place on top and sprinkle with some **watercress**, to finish.

Spread **1 heaping teaspoon of ricotta cheese** over **1 x 2½-oz slice of rye bread or toast**. Finely slice ½ **a ripe avocado** and **6 small ripe strawberries** and arrange on top, then scatter over **1 teaspoon of pine nuts**. Finish by drizzling with **1 teaspoon of thick balsamic vinegar**.

Spread **1 heaping teaspoon of ricotta cheese** over **1 x 2½-oz slice of rye bread or toast**. Finely slice and lay over ½ **a ripe avocado** and squeeze over a little **lemon juice**. In a dry pan, fry **1 rasher of smoked pancetta** until crispy, place on top of the avo, and sprinkle with a pinch of black pepper, to finish.

CALORIES	FAT	SAT FAT	PROTEIN	CARBS	SUGAR	SALT	FIBER
353kcal	16.5g	3.6g	12.2g	42.5g	5.7g	1.4g	6.8g

THESE VALUES ARE AN AVERAGE OF THE 18 RECIPES ON PAGES 38 TO 41

QUICK FIXES

Get-out-of-jail recipes you can get on
the table in 25 minutes, or less

CHICKEN LOLLIPOP DIPPERS
PEA & MINT COUSCOUS, CHARRED ASPARAGUS

— As well as being nice and high in fiber, humble whole-wheat couscous is high in the mineral copper, which our metabolic systems need in order to function efficiently —

SERVES 2

24 MINUTES

8 oz fine asparagus

¾ cup fresh or frozen peas

¾ cup whole-wheat couscous

1 lemon

¾ oz flaked almonds

2 x 4-oz boneless, skinless
  chicken breasts

olive oil

2 heaping teaspoons sun-dried
  tomato paste

2 tablespoons plain yogurt

½ a bunch of fresh mint (½ oz)

Trim six wooden skewers so they'll fit inside a large non-stick frying pan, then soak in cold water. Trim the woody ends off the asparagus, then char in the dry pan on a medium heat, turning occasionally. Meanwhile, place the peas and couscous in a bowl. Finely grate over the lemon zest, then just cover with boiling kettle water. Pop a plate on top and leave to fluff up.

Once done, remove the asparagus to the plate, crumble the almonds into the pan to toast until lightly golden, then remove. Use the base of a pan to flatten the thicker side of the chicken breasts slightly, then use three wooden skewers to pierce each chicken breast at regular intervals. Sprinkle both breasts with a pinch of sea salt and black pepper and rub with 1 teaspoon of oil. Place the chicken breasts in the pan for 10 minutes, or until golden and cooked through, but still juicy, turning every couple of minutes, and returning the asparagus to the pan for the last minute to warm through.

Meanwhile, mix the sun-dried tomato paste with the yogurt and half the lemon juice until smooth. Fluff up the couscous, squeeze over the remaining lemon juice, then pick, finely chop, and stir in the mint leaves. Taste and season to perfection. Slice between the skewers to create chicken lollipops ready to dunk in the sun-dried tomato yogurt and coat in the crunchy almonds, then serve up with the couscous and asparagus.

CALORIES	FAT	SAT FAT	PROTEIN	CARBS	SUGAR	SALT	FIBER	2 PORTIONS VEG & FRUIT
535kcal	15.7g	2.7g	46.2g	53.8g	8.2g	0.9g	7.9g	

JAPANESE MISO STEW
TOFU, SEAWEED, GREENS, & CHILI OIL

In small amounts (because of its high salt content), dried seaweed is super-nutritious. It's super-high in iodine, a mineral essential in ensuring our thyroid gland can function properly

SERVES 2

15 MINUTES

2 heaping teaspoons traditional
    white miso paste

1 handful of quality dried
    seaweed

4 scallions

5½ oz mixed green veg, such as
    broccolini, asparagus,
    bok choy, Chinese greens

5½ oz mixed exotic mushrooms

7 oz firm silken tofu

4½ oz dried brown rice noodles

1 lime

1 tablespoon chili oil

Pour 5 cups of boiling kettle water into a pan on a medium-high heat and stir in the miso and seaweed. Trim and finely slice the scallions. Prep your greens, trimming and halving any broccolini and asparagus spears lengthways, and cutting bok choy and Chinese greens into thin wedges. Add it all to the miso broth, adding the mushrooms whole or tearing them in, then cube up and stir in the tofu. Leave on the heat for 5 minutes, so everything is just cooked through but still full of life and color.

Meanwhile, cook the noodles according to the package instructions, then drain and stir into the broth. Have a taste, then tweak to perfection with squeezes of lime juice. Portion up and serve with a few drips of chili oil.

CALORIES	FAT	SAT FAT	PROTEIN	CARBS	SUGAR	SALT	FIBER	2 PORTIONS VEG & FRUIT
322kcal	13.2g	2.3g	20.1g	30.2g	3.5g	1.5g	7.8g	

PASTA PESTO
GREEN BEANS, BROCCOLINI, & ASPARAGUS

Swapping in whole-grain pasta can not only up your fiber intake here, but also gives us other essential micronutrients, including iron, which our brains need in order to function properly

SERVES 4

20 MINUTES

4 portions of super-quick batch pesto (see page 232)

1½ lbs mixed green veg—I use fine green beans, broccolini, and asparagus

10 oz dried whole-wheat rigatoni or penne

½ a lemon

2 sprigs of fresh basil

1 oz Parmesan cheese

If you haven't done it already, make up a batch of super-quick pesto (see page 232). Trim just the stalk ends off the green beans. Split the broccolini stalks in half, leaving the florets intact. Trim the woody ends off the asparagus, halving lengthways if the spears are thick. Cook the pasta in a large pan of boiling salted water according to the package instructions. Add the green beans 6 minutes before the pasta time is up, the broccolini 3 minutes before, and the asparagus just 2 minutes before. Drain the pasta and veg, reserving a cupful of cooking water.

Return the pasta and veg to the empty pan, add the pesto, and toss together well, loosening with a little reserved water, if needed. Plate up, then, from a height, grate over the lemon zest and scatter with picked basil leaves. Finely grate over the Parmesan and serve.

CALORIES	FAT	SAT FAT	PROTEIN	CARBS	SUGAR	SALT	FIBER	2 PORTIONS VEG & FRUIT
517kcal	23.1g	5.9g	25.3g	55.5g	6.9g	0.6g	10.5g	

SRI LANKAN SHRIMP CURRY
TAMARIND, BABY CORN, & PINEAPPLE RICE

— As well as lean shrimp giving us a nice hit of protein, they contain phosphorus, which is important for good bone health, as is manganese, which we get from the pineapple —

SERVES 6

25 MINUTES

2¼ cups basmati rice

1 x 16-oz can of pineapple chunks, in juice

2 red onions

1½-inch piece of fresh gingerroot

1–2 fresh red or yellow chiles

1 small handful of curry leaves

1 heaping teaspoon curry powder

2 heaping teaspoons black mustard seeds

2 heaping teaspoons tamarind paste

1 lb ripe tomatoes

1 x 14-oz can of light coconut milk

6 oz baby corn

1½ lbs large frozen peeled shrimp

6 tablespoons plain yogurt

Put the rice into a pan with double the volume of boiling salted water. Add the canned pineapple (juice and all), then cook with the lid on over a medium heat for 12 minutes, or until all the liquid has been absorbed, stirring occasionally.

Meanwhile, peel and dice the onions, peel and finely chop the ginger, and finely slice the chiles. Place a large non-stick casserole pan on a medium-high heat with the curry leaves, curry powder, and mustard seeds. A minute later, stir in the onions, ginger, and chiles with the tamarind paste and cook for 5 minutes, stirring regularly, and adding splashes of water to stop it sticking, if needed. Roughly chop and stir in the tomatoes, pour in the coconut milk, drop in the baby corn and shrimp, and bring to a boil. Pop the lid on and simmer for 8 to 10 minutes, or until the shrimp are cooked through. Serve the pineapple rice with the curry, adding a spoonful of yogurt to each portion.

-------------------- *Bonus flavor* --------------------

Fresh shell-on shrimp are easy to prep if you've got the confidence. Peel the shrimp, run your knife down the back of each one, so they butterfly as they cook, and remove the veins. Pull off the heads and chuck into the pan for added flavor, removing before you serve. A good fishmonger will do this prep for you.

CALORIES	FAT	SAT FAT	PROTEIN	CARBS	SUGAR	SALT	FIBER	2 PORTIONS
532kcal	8g	5g	31.1g	89.6g	17.5g	0.6g	3.5g	VEG & FRUIT

CHICKEN GOUJONS
PITA, LITTLE GEM, TOMATOES, & AVO SAUCE

— When ingredients work together to maximize their nutritional impact, we like that! Here, the fat in the avocado and oil helps us to absorb fat-soluble vitamin K from the lettuce —

SERVES 4

23 MINUTES

6 whole grain pita breads

4 x 4-oz boneless, skinless chicken breasts

1 bunch of fresh basil (1 oz)

1 large egg

2 cloves of garlic

¾ oz Parmesan cheese

1 lemon

4 heaping tablespoons Greek yogurt

1 ripe avocado

chipotle Tabasco sauce

extra virgin olive oil

2 little gem lettuces or hearts of romaine

11 oz ripe cherry tomatoes, on the vine

Preheat the oven to 400°F. Tear 2 pita breads into a blender and blitz into fine crumbs, then pour into a shallow tray. Slice the chicken lengthways into ½-inch strips and place in a large bowl. Add half the basil to the blender with the egg. Peel and add the garlic. Finely grate in the Parmesan and lemon zest, and squeeze in all the lemon juice. Add a pinch of sea salt and a good pinch of black pepper and blitz until smooth. Pour over the chicken and toss together well, massaging that flavor into the meat.

Working in batches, gently turn the chicken strips in the tray of crumbs until nicely coated. Place on a large baking sheet, then bake for 15 to 18 minutes, or until golden and cooked through, turning halfway.

Meanwhile, quickly rinse the blender, then put in most of the remaining basil and the yogurt. Peel, pit, and add the avocado, then blitz until smooth. Taste and season to perfection, then divide between your plates and add a few drips of chipotle Tabasco and oil to each portion. Lightly toast the remaining pitas, pick apart the little gem leaves, and halve the cherry tomatoes. Divide it all between your plates with the goujons, pick over the remaining basil leaves, mix it up, and tuck in.

Get ahead

Make the marinade, toss with the chicken, and leave overnight in the fridge so the flavors really penetrate, then coat in bread crumbs the next day.

CALORIES	FAT	SAT FAT	PROTEIN	CARBS	SUGAR	SALT	FIBER	2 PORTIONS VEG & FRUIT
520kcal	15.5g	5.2g	47.2g	48.3g	8.1g	1.5g	7.2g	

PASTA & 7-VEG TOMATO SAUCE
4 SUPER-SIMPLE WAYS – PART 1

We all love pasta with a good sauce—it's such an easy meal to knock together. Get into the spirit with these classic combos, and get ahead with my super-nutritious 7-veg tomato sauce

EACH SERVES 2

12 MINUTES

ASPARAGUS, PEA, & MINT

Cook **5 oz of dried whole-wheat penne** in a pan of boiling salted water according to the package instructions. Meanwhile, trim the woody ends off **1 bunch of asparagus (12 oz)**, cut into ¾-inch chunks, and fry in a large non-stick frying pan on a medium heat with **1 teaspoon of olive oil**. After 2 minutes, add **1 cup of frozen peas** and **1¼ cups of 7-veg tomato sauce** (see page 234) and simmer until the pasta is ready. Pick and finely chop the leaves from **2 sprigs of fresh mint** and finely grate **¾ oz of Parmesan cheese**. Drain the pasta, reserving a cupful of cooking water, then toss the pasta through the sauce with the chopped mint and grated Parmesan, loosening with a splash of the reserved water, if needed. Divide between your plates and tuck in.

BACON BITS, ROSEMARY, & BALSAMIC

Cook **5 oz of dried whole-wheat fusilli** in a pan of boiling salted water according to the package instructions. Meanwhile, finely slice **2 rashers of smoked bacon** and fry in a large non-stick frying pan on a medium heat with **1 teaspoon of olive oil** until golden. Add a pinch of black pepper, strip in the leaves from **2 sprigs of fresh rosemary**, then after 1 minute remove, leaving the fat behind. Add **1¼ cups of 7-veg tomato sauce** (see page 234) with **2 tablespoons of balsamic vinegar** and simmer until the pasta is ready. Drain the pasta, reserving a cupful of cooking water, then toss the pasta through the sauce, loosening with a splash of the reserved water, if needed. Divide up, finely grate over **¾ oz of Parmesan cheese**, and serve sprinkled with the crispy bits.

PASTA & 7-VEG TOMATO SAUCE
4 SUPER-SIMPLE WAYS – PART 2

Making the simple trade-up from regular white pasta to a whole-wheat variety can be a really
easy way to up our fiber intake, something many of us aren't getting enough of from day to day

EACH SERVES 2
12 MINUTES

RICOTTA, ARUGULA, & PINE NUTS

Cook **5 oz of dried whole-wheat spaghetti** in a pan of boiling salted water according to the package instructions.
Meanwhile, fry **2 tablespoons of ricotta cheese** in a large non-stick frying pan on a medium heat with **2 teaspoons
of olive oil**. Finely grate in the zest of **1 lemon**, add **2 tablespoons of pine nuts**, and fry for 1 minute. Add **1¼ cups
of 7-veg tomato sauce** (see page 234) and simmer until the pasta is ready. Drain the pasta, reserving a cupful of
cooking water, then toss the pasta through the sauce, loosening with a splash of the reserved water, if needed.
Divide between your plates, then sprinkle with a handful of lemon-dressed **arugula leaves**, to finish.

FLAKED TUNA, CAPERS, & LEMON

Cook **5 oz of dried pasta shells** in a pan of boiling salted water according to the package instructions. Meanwhile,
rinse **2 teaspoons of baby capers**, fry in a large non-stick frying pan on a medium heat with **1 teaspoon of olive
oil** and the finely grated zest of **1 lemon** until golden, then remove, leaving any oil behind. Add **1¼ cups of 7-veg
tomato sauce** (see page 234) and squeezes of lemon juice, to taste. Drain and flake in **1 x 6-oz can of tuna in
spring water**, add **1 pinch of ground cinnamon**, then stir through **2 tablespoons of cottage cheese** and simmer
until the pasta is ready. Drain the pasta, reserving a cupful of cooking water, then toss the pasta through the
sauce, loosening with a splash of the reserved water, if needed. Divide up, then sprinkle over the crispy bits.

CALORIES	FAT	SAT FAT	PROTEIN	CARBS	SUGAR	SALT	FIBER	2 PORTIONS VEG & FRUIT
419kcal	10g	3g	22g	64g	12g	1g	9g	

THESE VALUES ARE AN AVERAGE OF THE FOUR RECIPES ON PAGES 54 TO 56

VEGGIE FRIED RICE
SESAME, TOFU, & CHILI EGGS

As well as being super-versatile and a great source of veggie protein, tofu is high in calcium, which our blood needs to make the enzymes that we require to digest our food properly

SERVES 2

19 MINUTES

peanut oil

7 oz firm silken tofu

10 oz mixed exotic mushrooms

2 cloves of garlic

1½-inch piece of fresh gingerroot

4 scallions

5 oz sugar snap peas

1 x 8½-oz pack of ready-made
  brown basmati rice

2 heaping teaspoons raw sesame
  seeds

2 large eggs

hot chili sauce

1 tablespoon reduced-sodium
  soy sauce

1 lime

Place 1 teaspoon of peanut oil in a cold non-stick frying pan and put on a medium-high heat. Chop the tofu into 4 chunks, place in the pan, and leave to get golden. Place a large non-stick frying pan on a high heat alongside it. Pick through the mushrooms, halving any larger ones, and sprinkle into the pan to dry char for 5 minutes, so they get dark golden and beautifully nutty.

Meanwhile, peel and finely slice the garlic and ginger. Trim the scallions, finely slice just the top green halves and put aside, cutting the rest into ¾-inch chunks. Push the charred mushrooms to one side of the pan, add 1 tablespoon of peanut oil to the empty side, then toss the garlic, ginger, and white scallions in the oil. After 1 minute, toss all of that with the mushrooms, add the sugar snaps and the rice, and stir-fry for 5 minutes.

At the same time, turn the tofu over, sprinkle the sesame seeds into the pan, and crack in the eggs. Swirl the pan to spread the eggs, then scatter over the green scallions and drizzle with chili sauce. Cover and leave to cook through for 4 minutes. Toss the soy sauce through the veggie rice, then serve with the sesame tofu eggs, and lime wedges on the side, for squeezing over.

CALORIES	FAT	SAT FAT	PROTEIN	CARBS	SUGAR	SALT	FIBER	2 PORTIONS
514kcal	23.7g	5.3g	26.8g	51.8g	6.7g	0.9g	5.5g	VEG & FRUIT

GRILLED BEEF KEBABS
SHREDDED CRUNCH SALAD, FETA, & PITA

—   Beef gives us B vitamins here, which our metabolic and nervous systems need, while the   —
cabbage, mint, and pomegranate give us vitamin C, helping us absorb iron from the pita

SERVES 4

25 MINUTES

1 lb lean ground beef

1 large egg

1¾ oz dried cranberries

1¾ oz shelled unsalted pistachios

1 heaping teaspoon garam masala

olive oil

1 red onion

2 lemons

1 lb white and/or red cabbage

1 large carrot

1 pomegranate

½ a bunch of fresh mint (½ oz)

4 whole-grain pita breads

1 oz feta cheese

4 tablespoons plain yogurt

If using wooden skewers, soak them for a few minutes in cold water. Preheat the broiler to high. In a food processor, blitz the ground beef, egg, cranberries, pistachios, garam masala, and a pinch of sea salt and black pepper until well combined. Divide the mixture into four equal-sized portions, then use wet hands to scrunch and shape each portion around a wooden or metal skewer. Lay the skewers across an oiled pan. Pop under the grill for 10 minutes, or until golden and cooked through, turning halfway.

Peel and finely slice the onion, ideally on a mandolin (use the guard!) or using good knife skills, then toss in the lemon juice and a pinch of salt on a big platter. Remove and discard any tatty outer leaves from the cabbage, finely shred it, peel the carrot and finely matchstick lengthways, then pile both on top of the onion. Halve the pomegranate, then, holding one half cut-side down in your fingers, bash the back of it with a spoon so the seeds tumble onto the platter, and repeat with the other half. Pick, roughly chop, and scatter over the mint leaves, ready to toss together.

Lightly toast the pita breads until just warmed through, mix up the salad, and serve with the kebabs, a crumbling of feta cheese, and a dollop of yogurt.

CALORIES	FAT	SAT FAT	PROTEIN	CARBS	SUGAR	SALT	FIBER	2 PORTIONS
531kcal	18.3g	5.9g	40.2g	51.6g	22.7g	1.5g	9.1g	VEG & FRUIT

CHEAT'S PEA SOUP
SMOKY HAM, PASTA, MINT, & FETA

___ This super-speedy soup utilizes freezer staples peas and spinach, both of which give us __
vitamin C, helping us to absorb the all-important iron contained in the pasta

SERVES 4

24 MINUTES

1 bunch of scallions

2 cups frozen peas

10 oz frozen chopped spinach

3½ oz smoked ham

½ a bunch of fresh mint (½ oz)

10 oz dried whole-wheat fusilli

1¾ oz feta cheese

Trim the scallions and place in a blender with the frozen peas and spinach. Tear in the ham, pick in the mint leaves, then cover with 1⅔ cups of boiling kettle water. Put the lid on securely, cover with a kitchen towel, and, holding it in place, blitz until smooth, stopping to scrape down the sides and help it along, if needed. Pour into a large pan on a high heat and add another 5 cups of boiling kettle water. Smash up the pasta into random shapes—the easiest way is to wrap it in a kitchen towel and attack it with a rolling pin—and stir into the soup. Bring to a boil, then simmer until the pasta is cooked through, stirring regularly and adding splashes of water to loosen, if needed. Taste the soup, and season to perfection.

Divide the soup between bowls or mugs, then use a vegetable peeler to shave over the feta in fine strips, before tucking in.

CALORIES	FAT	SAT FAT	PROTEIN	CARBS	SUGAR	SALT	FIBER	2 PORTIONS
418kcal	9.1g	3.3g	26g	61.1g	10.1g	1.5g	11.8g	VEG & FRUIT

CRISPY TROUT, OATS, & THYME
HORSERADISH YOGURT, SPUDS, & VEG

__ Tasty trout is super-high in vitamin B$_{12}$, which we need for red blood cell production, in turn __
preventing us from feeling tired, plus we get a good hit of vitamin C from all the veggies

SERVES 2

21 MINUTES

14 oz baby white potatoes

5 oz small carrots

7 oz broccolini

1 cup frozen peas

2 teaspoons jarred grated
   horseradish

2 heaping tablespoons plain
   yogurt

1 lemon

2 x 4-oz trout fillets, scaled,
   pin-boned

olive oil

½ a bunch of fresh thyme (½ oz)

1 tablespoon rolled oats

Cook the baby potatoes in a large pan of boiling salted water for 15 to 20 minutes, or until cooked through. Wash or peel the carrots, halve lengthways, and add to the pan for the last 8 minutes. Trim the broccolini and add for the last 5 minutes, adding the peas for the last 2 minutes only. Mix the horseradish and yogurt with half the lemon juice and put aside.

With a few minutes to go, place a large non-stick frying pan on a medium-high heat. Drizzle the fish fillets with 1 teaspoon of oil and sprinkle with a pinch of sea salt and black pepper, then place in the pan flesh-side down for 2 minutes. Strip in the thyme leaves, sprinkle in the oats, then flip over and gently press down with a slotted spatula so the skin is in good contact with the pan. Cook for 4 to 6 minutes, or until the skin is super-crispy (depending on the shape of your fillets), then turn the heat off.

Drain the spuds and veg and divide between your plates. Lightly crush the spuds, making a bed of them on each plate, then sit the trout fillets proudly on top, skin-side up. Spoon over the horseradish yogurt, add a pinch of black pepper, and serve with lemon wedges, for squeezing over.

CALORIES	FAT	SAT FAT	PROTEIN	CARBS	SUGAR	SALT	FIBER	2 PORTIONS
479kcal	13.2g	3.6g	39.4g	53.6g	13.5g	1.1g	10.9g	VEG & FRUIT

PESTO MUSSELS & TOAST
BABY ZUCCHINI, SWEET TOMATOES, & PEAS

Mussels are a super-nutritious member of the shellfish family, packed with micronutrients, including iodine and selenium, two important minerals for healthy metabolic function

SERVES 2

14 MINUTES

2 portions of super-quick batch pesto (see page 232)

2 thick slices of whole-grain bread (1¾ oz each)

7 oz baby zucchini

7 oz ripe mixed-color cherry tomatoes, on the vine

1 lb mussels, scrubbed, debearded

1¼ cups fresh or frozen peas

optional: ¼ cup white wine

2 sprigs of fresh basil

If you haven't done it already, make up a batch of super-quick pesto (see page 232). Put a large pan on a medium-high heat, and toast the bread as the pan heats up, turning when golden. Trim and finely slice the zucchini, and halve the cherry tomatoes. Check the mussels—if any are open, just give them a little tap and they should close; if they don't they're no good, so chuck those ones away. Remove the toast and spread half a portion of pesto on each slice.

Turn the heat under the pan up to full whack and tip in the mussels. Stir in the remaining portion of pesto, the zucchini, tomatoes, and peas. Add the wine (if using), or a good splash of water. Cover with a lid and leave to steam for 3 to 4 minutes, shaking the pan occasionally. When all the mussels have opened and are soft and juicy, they're ready. If any remain closed, simply throw those away. Divide the mussels, veg, and all those gorgeous juices between two large bowls, pick over the basil leaves, and serve with the pesto toasts on the side for some epic dunking.

CALORIES	FAT	SAT FAT	PROTEIN	CARBS	SUGAR	SALT	FIBER	3 PORTIONS VEG & FRUIT
471kcal	22.1g	4.6g	30.8g	36.5g	11.7g	1.3g	8.7g	

SWEET & SOUR STIR-FRY
LOADSA SPROUTS, PINEAPPLE, & NOODLES

Sprouts are super-quick to cook, so they're brilliant in stir-fries like this, plus both alfalfa and beansprouts give us a good hit of folic acid, which our bodies need to make protein

SERVES 2

21 MINUTES

3½ oz fine rice noodles

1 x 8-oz can of pineapple chunks, in juice

2 heaping teaspoons cornstarch

1 tablespoon cider vinegar

2 teaspoons reduced-sodium soy sauce

2 teaspoons raw sesame seeds

1 oz unsalted cashew nuts

4 scallions

2 cloves of garlic

¾-inch piece of fresh gingerroot

1 fresh red chile

7 oz sugar snap peas

peanut oil

7 oz sprouts, such as alfalfa sprouts, chickpea sprouts, beansprouts

1 lime

In a bowl, cover the noodles with boiling kettle water to rehydrate them. To make a sauce, drain the pineapple juice into a separate bowl, mix with the cornstarch, vinegar, soy sauce, and 4 tablespoons of water, then put aside.

Put a wok or large frying pan on a high heat and lightly toast the sesame seeds while it heats up, then tip into a little bowl. Place the pineapple chunks in the dry pan, then roughly chop the cashew nuts and add a minute later. Trim the scallions, slice into ¾-inch chunks, and add to the pan. Let it all char and get attitude while you peel the garlic and ginger, finely slice them with the chile (seed if you like), and finely slice the sugar snaps at an angle lengthways. Add 1 tablespoon of peanut oil to the pan, then add the garlic, ginger, and chile. Toss for 30 seconds, then toss in the sugar snaps and the more robust sprouts for 1 minute, followed by the sauce. Bring it to a boil for a minute or two to thicken, then taste and season to perfection.

Serve the stir-fry on top of the drained noodles. Quickly return the empty pan to the heat, pour in a good splash of boiling kettle water, use a wooden spoon to really scrape up all that delicious sticky goodness from the bottom, stirring for 1 minute until slightly thickened, then drizzle over the stir-fry. Sprinkle over any delicate sprouts, such as alfalfa, along with the toasted sesame seeds, and serve with lime wedges, for squeezing over.

CALORIES	FAT	SAT FAT	PROTEIN	CARBS	SUGAR	SALT	FIBER	3 PORTIONS VEG & FRUIT
492kcal	16.7g	3.1g	14.8g	70.7g	20.4g	0.6g	4.4g	

CREAMY CHOPPED SALAD
GRAPES, TARRAGON, CHICKEN, & CROUTONS

All the veggies in this colorful salad ensure it's super-filling and packed with nutrients—both cucumber and lettuce have a high water content and give us a nice hit of vitamin K

SERVES 4

20 MINUTES

4 thick slices of whole-grain bread
  (1¾ oz each)

½ cup plain yogurt

1 bunch of fresh tarragon (1 oz)

extra virgin olive oil

2 oz jarred sliced jalapeño chiles

1 x 11-oz can of sweetcorn in
  water

2 large roasted peeled red
  peppers in brine

1 cucumber

1 iceberg lettuce

6 scallions

7 oz grapes

11 oz leftover poached chicken
  (see page 230)

1½ oz feta cheese

Preheat the oven to 350°F. Cut the bread into ¾-inch dice, arrange on a roasting pan in a single layer, and pop into the oven for 15 minutes, or until golden and nicely crisp, shaking occasionally.

Meanwhile, in a blender, blitz the yogurt, tarragon, 1 tablespoon of oil, the jalapeños, and 2 tablespoons of liquor from the jar until smooth. Taste and season to perfection. Tip the sweetcorn into a super-large bowl (juice and all), pour in the dressing, and mix together. Drain the peppers and chop into ½-inch dice, then add to the bowl. Halve the cucumber lengthways and scrape out the watery core, then slice it ¼ inch thick and add to the bowl. Halve the lettuce, then slice, cut into ¾-inch dice, and add to the bowl. Trim and finely slice the scallions, halve the grapes, then add those to the bowl, too.

Shred or chop your leftover chicken and gently toss into the bowl until everything is well coated in the creamy dressing. Mix in most of the crunchy croutons, then sprinkle the rest on top, crumble over the feta, and serve.

CALORIES	FAT	SAT FAT	PROTEIN	CARBS	SUGAR	SALT	FIBER	3 PORTIONS
475kcal	15.5g	4.9g	34.7g	47.3g	19.1g	1.3g	7g	VEG & FRUIT

SESAME BUTTERFLIED CHICKEN
PEANUT SAUCE, ASIAN SLAW, & RICE NOODLES

Adding a lovely bit of crunch to this simple dish, slaw ingredients Napa cabbage and sugar snap peas are a source of vitamin C, which we need to make cell-protecting vitamin E

SERVES 2

18 MINUTES

3½ oz fine rice noodles

2 x 4-oz boneless, skinless
   chicken breasts

peanut oil

4 scallions

½ a Napa cabbage (5 oz)

7 oz sugar snap peas

½–1 fresh red chile

2 limes

1 tablespoon reduced-sodium
   soy sauce

1 tablespoon peanut butter

2 tablespoons plain yogurt

¾-inch piece of fresh gingerroot

2 teaspoons raw sesame seeds

Put a grill pan on a high heat. In a bowl, cover the noodles with boiling kettle water to rehydrate them. Use a sharp knife to slice into the chicken breasts, then open each one out flat like a book. Rub each with 1 teaspoon of peanut oil and a small pinch of sea salt and black pepper, then grill for 8 minutes, or until golden and cooked through, turning halfway.

Trim the scallions and rattle them through the finest slicer on your food processor, followed by the Napa cabbage, sugar snap peas, and chile. Dress with the juice of 1 lime and the soy sauce. In a small bowl, mix the peanut butter with the yogurt and the juice of the remaining lime, peel and finely grate in the ginger, mix again, taste, and season to perfection.

Remove the chicken to a board and slice, lightly toasting the sesame seeds in the residual heat of the grill pan and sprinkling them over the chicken before serving. Drain the noodles, divide between your plates with the chicken, slaw, and peanut sauce, mix it all up and tuck on in.

CALORIES	FAT	SAT FAT	PROTEIN	CARBS	SUGAR	SALT	FIBER	2 PORTIONS
489kcal	12.9g	3.3g	40g	52g	8.5g	1.3g	3.3g	VEG & FRUIT

HEALTHY CLASSICS

All our ultimate comfort food classics,

freshened up super-food style

SUPER SHEPHERD'S PIE
SMASHED NEEPS & TATTIES

—   Lean ground lamb works a treat here, and gives us a bumper hit of vitamin B12, keeping   —
our immune and nervous systems healthy and preventing a drop in our energy levels

SERVES 6

2 HOURS 15 MINUTES

1 lb lean ground lamb

2 sprigs of fresh rosemary

1 x 15-oz can of cannellini beans

2 onions

2 carrots

2 stalks of celery

8 oz chestnut or cremini
mushrooms

1 heaping tablespoon all-purpose
flour

3¼ cups chicken or veg stock

1¾ lbs rutabaga

1¾ lbs potatoes

2 tablespoons reduced-fat (2%)
milk

½ oz sharp Cheddar cheese

1 tablespoon Worcestershire sauce

1 teaspoon mint sauce

3½ cups frozen peas

Put the ground lamb into a cold casserole pan. Place on a high heat, add a really good pinch of black pepper, and cook for 15 minutes, or until dark golden, breaking it up with a wooden spoon. Pick and finely chop the rosemary leaves, drain the beans, then stir both into the pan. Cook and stir for 8 minutes, or until the beans start to pop and it's all getting dark and gnarly. Peel the onions and carrots, trim the celery, wipe the mushrooms clean, then finely chop it all (or blitz in a food processor). Stir into the pan and sweat for 10 minutes on a medium-high heat, stirring occasionally. Stir in the flour, followed by the stock. Bring to a boil, then simmer on a low heat with the lid on for 30 minutes.

Meanwhile, preheat the oven to 350°F. Wash the rutabaga and potatoes (leaving the skins on for extra nutritional benefit) and cut into 1¼-inch chunks. Cook just the rutabaga in a large pan of boiling salted water for 10 minutes, add the potatoes for 10 more minutes, or until cooked through, drain well, mash with the milk and grated cheese, and season to perfection.

Check the consistency of the ground lamb—you want it slightly wetter than you think, as it will thicken further in the oven. Add the Worcestershire and mint sauces, taste, and season to perfection. Sprinkle the peas over the ground lamb, letting them sit on the surface to help prevent the mash from sinking in too much. Put spoons of mash randomly on top, using a fork to scuff it up and make valleys and mountains, increasing the surface area and the crispy bits. Bake for 50 minutes, or until golden and bubbling. Nice with seasonal greens.

CALORIES	FAT	SAT FAT	PROTEIN	CARBS	SUGAR	SALT	FIBER	4 PORTIONS
436kcal	12.2g	5g	31.2g	51.2g	15.2g	0.4g	11.8g	VEG & FRUIT

ITALIAN SUPER-FOOD BURGERS
BALSAMIC ONIONS, MOZZARELLA, & SLAW

— The secret here is to use lean ground beef, which is just as protein-packed as the higher-fat stuff, bulked up with high-fiber cannellini beans. We even get a bit of mozzarella, too! —

SERVES 6
40 MINUTES

2 small red onions

6 tablespoons cheap balsamic vinegar

1 lb lean ground beef

1 x 15-oz can of cannellini beans

1 large egg

6 whole-grain buns

2 tablespoons raw sesame seeds

½ a small white cabbage (1 lb)

3 tablespoons plain yogurt

1 heaping teaspoon English mustard

1 teaspoon dried red chili flakes

1 lemon

olive oil

1 x 4-oz ball of mozzarella cheese

2 sprigs of fresh rosemary

2 ripe mixed-color tomatoes

3½ oz arugula

Preheat the oven to 400°F. Peel the onions, finely slice into rounds, and place in a bowl. Add the balsamic and a couple of good pinches of sea salt to draw out excess moisture (you'll drain the liquor off, so don't worry about the amount of salt).

Put the ground beef into a bowl with a big pinch of black pepper and a small pinch of salt. Drain and add the beans. Separate the egg and add the yolk to the mixture, then scrunch together really well with clean hands. Whisk the egg white, halve your burger buns, put back together, brush just the tops with egg white, then scatter over the sesame seeds to create a nice, even layer (you can even make stencils for a bit of fun, if you want to get the kids involved).

Pull off any tatty outer leaves from the cabbage. Very finely slice it, ideally on a mandolin (use the guard!). In a large bowl, toss the cabbage with the yogurt, mustard, chili flakes, lemon juice, and a pinch of black pepper.

Divide the burger mixture into six equal-sized balls. Place two large non-stick ovenproof frying pans on a medium-high heat with 1 teaspoon of oil in each (or cook in batches). Add three balls of mixture to each pan, gently squash into patties about ¾ inch thick, cook for 2 minutes, or until golden, then flip over. Top each burger with a slice of mozzarella and strip in the rosemary leaves around them. Pop into the oven for 2 minutes so the mozzarella melts, with the buns alongside to warm through. Slice the tomatoes and divide between the bun bases with the cheesy burgers, crispy rosemary, and balsamic onions, then pop the tops on, toss the slaw with the arugula, and serve.

CALORIES	FAT	SAT FAT	PROTEIN	CARBS	SUGAR	SALT	FIBER	2 PORTIONS VEG & FRUIT
446kcal	15.6g	6g	34.5g	38.9g	11.3g	1.5g	10g	

CHICKEN FAJITAS
SMOKY DRESSED EGGPLANTS & PEPPERS

— Sticking to super-lean chicken breasts is the key to making super-food fajitas, and also —
provides us with a great source of protein, ensuring our muscles stay strong and healthy

SERVES 4

40 MINUTES
PLUS MARINATING

olive oil

1 tablespoon red wine vinegar

1 teaspoon chipotle Tabasco
sauce

1 teaspoon dried oregano

2 teaspoons sweet smoked
paprika

2 cloves of garlic

1 large red onion

2 x 7-oz boneless, skinless
chicken breasts

3 mixed-color peppers

1 large eggplant

2 limes

1 bunch of fresh cilantro (1 oz)

1 ripe avocado

4 large whole-grain tortillas
with seeds

1¾ oz feta cheese

Put 1 tablespoon of oil into a bowl with the vinegar, chipotle Tabasco, oregano, paprika, and a pinch of sea salt and black pepper. Crush in the unpeeled garlic through a garlic crusher and mix together. Peel and halve the onion, slice into ½-inch-thick wedges, then slice the chicken lengthways ½ inch thick and toss both in the marinade. Leave in the fridge for at least 1 hour, or preferably overnight.

Blacken the whole peppers and eggplant over a direct flame on the stove, or in a grill pan on a high heat, until charred and blistered all over. Pop the peppers into a bowl and cover with plastic wrap for 10 minutes, then scrape off most of the black skin, discarding the stalks and seeds. Pinch the skin off the eggplant and trim off the ends. Nicely slice it all ¾ inch thick, dress on a platter with the juice of 1 lime and a few picked cilantro leaves, then taste and season to perfection.

Cook the chicken and onions in all that lovely marinade in a large non-stick frying pan on a medium-high heat for 6 to 8 minutes, or until cooked through, turning halfway. Peel, pit, and finely slice the avocado, and squeeze over the juice of half a lime. Warm the tortillas in a dry frying pan for 30 seconds, then keep warm in a clean kitchen towel. Take it all to the table, with the feta and the remaining cilantro leaves, and let everyone build their own.

CALORIES	FAT	SAT FAT	PROTEIN	CARBS	SUGAR	SALT	FIBER	2 PORTIONS
448kcal	16.4g	5.1g	34.1g	39.4g	11.1g	1.5g	10.7g	VEG & FRUIT

SALMON & SHRIMP FISH PIE
SWEET POTATO & SPUD MASH

—— Both salmon and shrimp are super-high in vitamin B$_{12}$, which we need for psychological ——
function, meaning so we can think properly, and salmon is a source of heart-healthy fats, too

SERVES 6

1 HOUR 20 MINUTES

1 rasher of smoked bacon

olive oil

1 large carrot

1 bunch of scallions

½ a bunch of fresh Italian
   parsley (½ oz)

2 tablespoons all-purpose flour

2½ cups reduced-fat (2%) milk

2 teaspoons English mustard

14 oz frozen chopped spinach

4 x 4-oz salmon fillets, skin off,
   pin-boned

7 oz raw peeled shrimp

3 cups frozen peas

4 oz feta cheese

1¼ lbs sweet potatoes

1¼ lbs potatoes

Preheat the oven to 350°F. Finely slice the bacon and place in a large roasting pan (14 x 12 inches) with 1 teaspoon of oil, then put on a medium heat (starting from cold helps the fat to render out of the bacon). Wash and trim the carrot and scallions, chop into ½-inch dice, and once the bacon is lightly golden, stir them into the pan. Finely slice and stir in the parsley stalks. Cook for 10 minutes, to soften, stirring regularly, then stir in the flour. Gradually pour in the milk, bring up to a good simmer, then stir in the mustard and frozen spinach. Simmer for 5 to 10 minutes, or until the spinach has thawed. Chop the salmon into bite-sized chunks, halve the shrimp, finely chop the parsley leaves, and stir it all through the sauce with the frozen peas, then crumble the feta over the top and turn the heat off.

Meanwhile, wash the sweet potatoes and spuds (leaving the skins on for extra nutritional benefit) and chop into 1¼-inch chunks. Cook in a large pan of boiling salted water for 15 minutes, or until cooked through, then drain and mash well, taste, and season to perfection. Gently spoon the mash over the fish pie filling, spreading it out with a fork. Bake for 40 minutes, or until golden and crisp on top, and bubbling at the edges.

CALORIES	FAT	SAT FAT	PROTEIN	CARBS	SUGAR	SALT	FIBER	3 PORTIONS VEG & FRUIT
537kcal	17.8g	6g	39g	58.2g	16g	1.5g	9.6g	

HEALTHY CHIP BUTTY
CHEESY SWEET POTATO, AVO, & KETCHUP

Using higher-fiber whole-grain bread and making a vitamin C–packed, reduced-sodium ketchup free from added sugar gives the typically calorie-and-salt-laden chip butty a super-food makeover

SERVES 2
40 MINUTES

1 large sweet potato (12 oz)

olive oil

1 tablespoon cider vinegar

1 tablespoon ground almonds

⅓ oz Cheddar cheese

3 ripe tomatoes

2 teaspoons chipotle Tabasco sauce

½ a bunch of fresh basil (½ oz)

½ a ripe avocado

½ a lime

2 heaping tablespoons plain yogurt

4 thin slices of whole-grain bread (1⅓ oz each)

Preheat the oven to 400°F. Wash the sweet potato (leaving the skin on for extra nutritional benefit) and cut into eighths. On a roasting pan, toss with 1 tablespoon of oil, the vinegar, and a small pinch of sea salt, then arrange in one layer and bake for 30 minutes, or until golden and cooked through. Sprinkle over the almonds, finely grate over the cheese, then return to the oven for 5 more minutes.

Meanwhile, score a cross in the skin of each tomato and cover with boiling kettle water in a bowl. After 2 minutes, drain, carefully pinch off the skins, then quarter and seed. Place the flesh in a pan on a medium-low heat with 1 tablespoon of oil and the chipotle Tabasco. Simmer gently for 15 minutes, or until thick, sweet, and delicious, stirring occasionally.

Pick the basil leaves into a pestle and mortar and pound with a pinch of sea salt. Peel, pit, and bash in the avo, then muddle in a squeeze of lime juice and the yogurt. Spread the avo mixture across all the slices of bread, like butter, then dollop the tomato on two of the slices. Line up your gnarly crispy cheesy sweet potato chips on top, pop the other slices on, and tuck in!

CALORIES	FAT	SAT FAT	PROTEIN	CARBS	SUGAR	SALT	FIBER	2 PORTIONS VEG & FRUIT
582kcal	26.4g	5.5g	14.9g	71.4g	18.5g	1.5g	7g	

CHICKEN TACOS
BLACK BEANS, AVO, CORN, & CHERRY TOMS

— Both black beans and flour are high in iron, which our bodies need for cognitive function— that's basically every intellectual process in our brains, from memory to reasoning

SERVES 4

30 MINUTES

1½ cups all-purpose whole-grain flour

olive oil

1 teaspoon cumin seeds

1 x 15-oz can of black beans

1 bunch of scallions

1 bunch of fresh cilantro (1 oz)

1 ripe avocado

2 corn on the cob

11 oz leftover poached chicken (see page 230)

7½ oz ripe cherry tomatoes, on the vine

2 limes

1 x 7-oz jar of sliced jalapeño chiles

4 heaping tablespoons plain yogurt

In a bowl, mix the flour with 1 tablespoon of oil, ⅔ cup of water, and a pinch of sea salt, then knead on a clean flour-dusted surface until smooth. Divide into twelve equal-sized balls and cover with a clean, damp kitchen towel.

Dry toast the cumin seeds in a small pan on a medium heat for 1 minute, then tip in the black beans (juice and all). Simmer on a low heat while you crack on with everything else, mashing once soft and loosening with a splash of water, if needed. Trim the scallions and finely slice with the cilantro stalks. Peel and pit the avocado, dice the flesh, and cut the corn kernels off the cobs. Heat it all in a large frying pan on a medium-low heat with 1 tablespoon of oil. Chop and add the chicken, stirring occasionally until ready to serve.

Quarter the cherry tomatoes and dress with the juice of 1 lime. In a blender, blitz the jalapeños and all their liquor with most of the cilantro leaves until super-smooth, then pour back into the jar (you'll only need 1 teaspoon per portion, so once done, simply pop the rest into the fridge for future meals).

Put a non-stick frying pan on the highest heat. Roll one of the dough balls out nice and thin into a rough circle (6 inches in diameter) and cook for just 20 seconds on each side, so it's soft and flexible. Roll the next one out while the previous one is cooking, stacking them in aluminum foil as you go so they stay warm and everyone can tuck in together (or you can serve them up to your lucky diners as you go, for a more authentic experience). Take everything to the table with the yogurt and lime wedges, and let everyone build their own.

CALORIES	FAT	SAT FAT	PROTEIN	CARBS	SUGAR	SALT	FIBER	2 PORTIONS VEG & FRUIT
600kcal	22.6g	5.2g	39.9g	60.7g	8.2g	0.8g	14.3g	

SMOKY VEGGIE CHILI
SWEET GEM & CHEESY BAKED SPUDS

_ Using cocoa powder helps to add a lovely depth of flavor here, and nutritionally it's high in _
the mineral copper, which we need to keep our skin and hair strong and healthy

SERVES 8
1 HOUR 45 MINUTES

2 onions

olive oil

1 heaping teaspoon cumin seeds

2 heaping teaspoons smoked
  paprika

2 teaspoons quality cocoa powder

1 heaping tablespoon peanut
  butter

1–2 fresh red chiles

3 large mixed-color peppers

2 sweet potatoes (10 oz each)

1 bunch of fresh cilantro (1 oz)

2 x 15-oz cans of butter beans

3 x 14-oz cans of plum tomatoes

8 small baking potatoes

5 oz Cheddar cheese

4 little gem lettuces or hearts
  of romaine

8 tablespoons plain yogurt

Put a large casserole pan on a medium-low heat and a grill pan beside it on a high heat. The idea here is to work in batches, starting by charring the veg on the grill to add a smoky flavor dimension. Peel the onions and cut into ½-inch dice, char on the grill for 3 minutes, then place in the casserole pan with 2 tablespoons of oil, the cumin seeds, paprika, cocoa, and peanut butter, stirring occasionally. Slice the chile(s) ½ inch thick and grill while you seed and roughly chop the peppers and chop the sweet potatoes into rough ¾-inch chunks (leave the skin on for extra nutritional benefit, just give them a wash). Grill it all, adding to the casserole pan as you go. Finely chop and add the cilantro stalks.

Preheat the oven to 350°F. Drain the beans in a sieve over the casserole pan so the juices go in, then tip the beans into the grill pan in an even layer. Have faith and leave them without stirring until they start to char and burst, then add to the veg. Pour in the canned tomatoes, breaking them up with a wooden spoon. Stir well, then pop the lid on ajar and leave for 1 hour, or until thickened, stirring occasionally. Meanwhile, wash the potatoes, prick, then bake for 1 hour, or until crispy on the outside, fluffy in the middle.

Just before serving, finely chop the cilantro leaves and stir through the chili, taste, and season to perfection. Cut a cross into each spud, pinching the bottoms so they open up, then grate the cheese and divide it between them, stuffing it in well. Pick apart the gem lettuces, and serve each cheesy spud with a good portion of chili, some gem leaves, and a dollop of yogurt.

CALORIES	FAT	SAT FAT	PROTEIN	CARBS	SUGAR	SALT	FIBER	5 PORTIONS VEG & FRUIT
445kcal	14.2g	5.8g	17.9g	65.1g	18.1g	0.7g	11g	

HEALTHY CHICKEN KIEV
BABY POTATOES, CARROTS, & GREEN VEG

I've given a family favorite, classic chicken Kiev, a super-food makeover by replacing the
usual butter in the filling with lighter cream cheese, giving a super-satisfying result

SERVES 4

45 MINUTES

1 clove of garlic

1¾ oz light cream cheese

1 lemon

1 oz Parmesan cheese

4 sprigs of fresh Italian parsley

4 x 4-oz boneless, skinless
  chicken breasts

2 slices of whole-grain bread
  (1¾ oz each)

olive oil

⅓ cup all-purpose flour

1 large egg

1½ lbs baby white potatoes

1½ lbs mixed veg, such as small
  carrots, peas, broccolini,
  sugar snap peas

extra virgin olive oil

Preheat the oven to 400°F. To make your filling, crush the unpeeled garlic through a garlic crusher into a small bowl with the cream cheese. Finely grate in the lemon zest and ¼ oz of the Parmesan, then add a little squeeze of lemon juice. Finely chop and add the parsley leaves, mix together well, then taste and season to perfection. Cut a deep pocket in the thickest part of each chicken breast. Divide up the filling, spoon into each pocket, then press the edges together to seal.

In a food processor, blitz the bread into crumbs with the remaining Parmesan and 1 tablespoon of olive oil, then tip into a shallow pan. Put the flour on a plate, and whisk the egg in a shallow bowl. One by one, coat the stuffed chicken in flour, shake off any excess, then gently drop into the beaten egg. Let any excess drip off, then turn and press in the crumbs until well coated all over. Repeat with the remaining breasts (you can keep these covered in the fridge for a couple of days, if you want to make them in advance). Place on a baking sheet and cook for 30 minutes, or until golden and cooked through.

Meanwhile, cook the baby potatoes in a large pan of boiling salted water for 15 to 20 minutes, or until tender. Wash or peel the carrots, halve lengthways, and add for the last 8 minutes, steaming your greens in a colander above the pan for 5 to 10 minutes, depending on what you're using. Drain it all and steam dry for 2 minutes, toss in a large bowl with 1 tablespoon of extra virgin olive oil and the remaining lemon juice, then season to perfection. Divide all the veg between your plates and serve with the Kievs.

CALORIES	FAT	SAT FAT	PROTEIN	CARBS	SUGAR	SALT	FIBER	2 PORTIONS VEG & FRUIT
527kcal	16.4g	4.9g	45.7g	50.9g	7.5g	0.8g	8.4g	

SWEET POTATO FISHCAKES
CHOPPED SALAD, FETA, & RED PEPPER SALSA

_ White fish is a great choice here, as it's both low in fat and super-nutritious. Haddock, _
for example, is packed full of iodine, which we need to support healthy brain function

SERVES 4

1 HOUR 10 MINUTES

1 lb potatoes

1 lb sweet potatoes

2 red peppers

extra virgin olive oil

2 teaspoons chipotle Tabasco
  sauce

1 lb white fish fillets, skin off,
  pin-boned

olive oil

1 cucumber

1 iceberg lettuce

1 heaping teaspoon English
  mustard

4 heaping tablespoons plain
  yogurt

1 tablespoon white wine vinegar

1½ oz feta cheese

½ a bunch of fresh mint (½ oz)

1 lemon

Wash the potatoes and sweet potatoes (leaving the skins on for extra nutritional benefit), chop into 1¼-inch chunks, and cook in a pan of boiling salted water for 15 minutes, or until cooked through. Drain, leave to steam dry and cool, then mash. Meanwhile, blacken the peppers over a direct flame on the stove or in a grill pan on a high heat, turning until charred and blistered all over. Pop into a bowl and cover with plastic wrap for 10 minutes, then scrape off most of the black skin, discarding the stalks and seeds. Finely chop, dress with 1 tablespoon of extra virgin olive oil and the chipotle Tabasco, then put aside.

Chop the fish into ½-inch dice, then mix into the cool mash really well with a pinch of sea salt and black pepper. Divide the mixture into eight even-sized balls and pat into 1¼-inch-thick patties. Put two large non-stick frying pans on a medium-low heat with 1 tablespoon of olive oil in each (or cook in batches). Cook four fishcakes in each pan, for 5 minutes on each side, or until golden and cooked through, carefully turning with a slotted spatula. If they break or crack a little, don't stress—these are light, chunky, rough-and-ready fishcakes.

Meanwhile, peel the cucumber, halve lengthways, and scrape out the watery core, then slice ¼ inch thick. Remove any tatty outer leaves from the iceberg, and roughly chop it into ½-inch chunks. In a bowl, dress both with the mustard, yogurt, and vinegar, mixing well, then taste, season to perfection, and crumble over the feta. Pick, roughly chop, and stir through most of the mint leaves. Serve the fishcakes and salsa scattered with baby mint leaves, with a good portion of salad and wedges of lemon, for squeezing over.

CALORIES	FAT	SAT FAT	PROTEIN	CARBS	SUGAR	SALT	FIBER	3 PORTIONS
423kcal	8.6g	2.7g	32.5g	56.9g	16g	7g	8.4g	VEG & FRUIT

CHEAT'S PIZZETTA
FENNEL, ARUGULA, & PROSCIUTTO

On those days when nothing else will do, this super-quick cheat's pizzetta will give us that comforting vibe, while using half whole-grain flour means we are upping our fiber intake

SERVES 2

25 MINUTES

heaping ¾ cup whole-grain self-rising flour

heaping ¾ cup self-rising flour, plus extra for dusting

6 tablespoons 7-veg tomato sauce (see page 234)

½ a zucchini

½ x 4-oz ball of mozzarella cheese

optional: 1 fresh red chile

1 small bulb of fennel (8 oz)

1¾ oz arugula

1 lemon

extra virgin olive oil

2 slices of prosciutto

1 tablespoon balsamic vinegar

Preheat the grill to high. Put an ovenproof frying pan on a high heat. Place the flours in a bowl with a pinch of sea salt, and gradually pour in up to ⅔ cup of water, stirring as you go so it comes together into a ball of dough. Knead for just 1 minute on a clean flour-dusted surface, then halve the dough and roll one piece out just under ½ inch thick. Place in the dry pan, then gently press your fingertips into the dough to create dimples. Cook for 3 minutes, or until the bottom starts to get golden, while you spread over half the 7-veg sauce. Very finely slice the zucchini into rounds and arrange half the slices over the pizzetta. Tear over half the mozzarella and add a few slices of chile (if using). Transfer the pan to the grill for 4 to 5 minutes, or until golden and bubbling.

Meanwhile, trim and finely slice the fennel, ideally on a mandolin or using a box grater. Toss with the arugula, half the lemon juice, and 2 teaspoons of oil in a bowl. Divide between two plates, wrapping a piece of prosciutto around each pile of salad. Take your pizzetta out of the oven and plate up, then drizzle over half the balsamic and add a wedge of lemon on the side. Serve up to your lucky companion, while you crack on with the second one.

- - - - - - - - - - - - - - *Veggie swap in* - - - - - - - - - - - - - - -
Lose the prosciutto and simply add a sprinkling of pine nuts under the cheese, so you still get a hit of protein.

CALORIES	FAT	SAT FAT	PROTEIN	CARBS	SUGAR	SALT	FIBER	2 PORTIONS
516kcal	13.4g	5.5g	23.6g	79.9g	10.9g	1.5g	7.3g	VEG & FRUIT

RATATOUILLE PIE
PHYLLO, RICOTTA, BASIL, & ALMONDS

Almonds provide our protein hit here, and as well as being packed with micronutrients they are a source of unsaturated fats, keeping our blood cholesterol and, in turn, our hearts healthy

SERVES 4

1 HOUR 20 MINUTES

olive oil

2 red onions

2 mixed-color peppers

2 zucchini

1 large eggplant

2 cloves of garlic

4 black olives (with pits)

2 x 14-oz cans of plum tomatoes

½ a bunch of fresh basil (½ oz)

6 sheets of phyllo pastry (8½ oz)

8 oz ricotta cheese

1¾ oz ground almonds

Preheat the oven to 350°F. Put a large, wide casserole pan on a high heat with 1 tablespoon of oil. Peel the onions, seed the peppers, trim the zucchini and eggplant, then chop it all into rough 1¼-inch chunks, adding them to the pan as you go. Peel, finely slice, and add the garlic. Squash the olives and remove the pits, then tear the flesh into the pan. Cook for 20 minutes, stirring regularly, to cook out the residual moisture. Pour in the canned tomatoes and bring to a boil, breaking up the tomatoes with a wooden spoon. Simmer vigorously for 15 minutes, or until thick in texture, then pick and stir through the basil leaves, taste, and season to perfection.

Working fairly quickly, wipe a drizzle of oil around the inside of a 10-inch pie dish. Layer up four sheets of phyllo, overlapping them and letting them hang over the edges of the dish. Spoon in the ratatouille, then randomly spoon over the ricotta and sprinkle in three-quarters of the almonds. Lightly scrunch up the remaining two sheets of phyllo and place on top, then fold in the overhanging pastry, scrunching it nicely. Sprinkle over the remaining almonds and bake for 40 to 45 minutes at the bottom of the oven, or until golden and crisp. Serve with a lemon-dressed seasonal salad on the side.

CALORIES	FAT	SAT FAT	PROTEIN	CARBS	SUGAR	SALT	FIBER	5 PORTIONS
505kcal	19.8g	5.8g	21.8g	60.2g	19.8g	1.1g	9g	VEG & FRUIT

SALADS

Epic super-food salads full of color,
texture, and incredible flavor

SUPER TUNA PASTA SALAD
FETA & CRISPY CAYENNE CRUMBS

Tuna gives us a hit of vitamin D, which in turn helps our bodies to absorb calcium from the feta cheese and plain yogurt, and they're what makes this salad creamy and delicious

SERVES 4

25 MINUTES

1 small red onion

2 lemons

8 oz dried pasta shells

12 oz broccoli

1 slice of whole-grain bread
   (1¾ oz)

½ teaspoon cayenne pepper

1 cucumber

½ a bunch of fresh chives or
   dill (½ oz)

4 tablespoons plain yogurt

2 x 6-oz cans of tuna in spring
   water

1¾ oz feta cheese

Peel and finely chop the onion, place in a large bowl with a pinch of sea salt and black pepper, then squeeze over all the lemon juice and put aside.

Cook the pasta in a large pan of boiling salted water according to the package instructions. Chop the broccoli florets off the stalk. Cut the woody end off the stalk, halve the stalk lengthways, then chuck it in with the pasta to cook through. Chop the florets into small bite-sized chunks, adding them to the water for the last minute only, just to take the rawness away.

Meanwhile, whiz the bread and cayenne into crumbs in a food processor, then toast in a dry non-stick frying pan on a medium heat until golden and crispy, tossing regularly. Peel the cucumber, halve lengthways and scrape out the watery core, then finely slice. Finely chop the herbs. Mix the yogurt into the lemony onion, then add the cucumber and herbs. Drain the pasta and broccoli, finely chop the broccoli stalk, and add it all to the bowl of dressing. Drain and flake in the tuna, toss together well, then taste and season to perfection. Divide between your bowls, and serve sprinkled with crumbled feta and the hot crispy crumbs.

CALORIES	FAT	SAT FAT	PROTEIN	CARBS	SUGAR	SALT	FIBER	2 PORTIONS
411kcal	6.2g	2.7g	33g	58.9g	8.8g	1.5g	6.4g	VEG & FRUIT

TANDOORI CHICKEN SALAD
MINTY YOGURT DRESSING & PAPPADAMS

Pantry staple brown rice is a fantastically nutritious base to this recipe—it's a bumper source of vitamins and minerals, including selenium for efficient immune system function

SERVES 4

45 MINUTES

4 x 4-oz boneless, skinless
  chicken breasts

4 teaspoons tandoori curry paste

1⅓ cups brown rice

1 small red onion

1 tablespoon white wine vinegar

½ a bunch of fresh mint (½ oz)

1 fresh red chile

4 heaping tablespoons plain
  yogurt

2 lemons

1 tablespoon black mustard seeds

1 teaspoon cumin seeds

14 oz ripe mixed-color cherry
  tomatoes, on the vine

2 carrots

2 little gem lettuces or hearts
  of romaine

4 uncooked pappadams

Lightly score a criss-cross pattern into both sides of each chicken breast, rub with the tandoori paste and a pinch of sea salt, massaging that flavor into the meat, then put aside. Cook the rice in a large pan of boiling salted water according to the package instructions, then drain and leave to steam dry in a large bowl. Peel and halve the red onion, and slice as finely as you can. In a bowl, scrunch it with the vinegar and a pinch of sea salt.

Rip the top leafy half of the mint into a blender, roughly slice and add the chile, add the yogurt and the juice of 1 lemon, pour in the liquor from the onion, then blitz until smooth and pour back over the onion. Toast the mustard and cumin seeds in a large non-stick frying pan on a medium-high heat, and add to the dressing. Dry fry the chicken in one layer for 4 minutes on each side, or until nicely charred, adding the remaining lemon halves alongside when you turn it. Once done, remove the chicken to a plate, carefully squeeze over the jammy lemon juice, rest for a couple of minutes, then slice.

Halve or quarter the cherry tomatoes and add to the rice bowl. Peel the carrots, and continue to peel into ribbons, adding to the bowl. Pour in the onion and dressing, toss it all together, taste and season to perfection, then pile in the center of a big platter. Trim the lettuces, click apart the leaves, and arrange around the salad with the slices of chicken. One by one, puff up the dry pappadams in the microwave for 30 seconds each, then crack and crumble them over the top of the salad and tuck in.

CALORIES	FAT	SAT FAT	PROTEIN	CARBS	SUGAR	SALT	FIBER	2 PORTIONS VEG & FRUIT
507kcal	10.3g	2.2g	39.3g	70.5g	12g	1.5g	5.7g	

JAMIE'S ITALIAN SUPER-FOOD SALAD
GRAINS, GRILLED AVO, BROCCOLINI, & HARISSA

Quinoa and black rice provide a deliciously nutty gluten-free base to this super salad, plus we get heart-healthy unsaturated fats from the seeds in the crunchy sprinkle

SERVES 4

30 MINUTES

1 cup quinoa

½ cup black rice

½ x 15-oz can of Puy lentils

½ x 15-oz can of chickpeas

½ a bulb of fennel

8 oz vac-packed or freshly
   cooked beets

1¾ oz kale

½ a bunch of fresh Italian
   parsley (½ oz)

½ a bunch of fresh mint (½ oz)

1 tablespoon sherry vinegar

extra virgin olive oil

2 ripe avocados

3½ oz broccolini

5 oz cottage cheese

4 teaspoons harissa

1¾ oz mixed seeds

½ a pomegranate

Cook the quinoa and rice in pans of boiling salted water according to the package instructions, then drain. Drain the lentils and chickpeas, and toss with the quinoa and rice in a large bowl. Finely slice the fennel, ideally on a mandolin (use the guard!), drain and quarter the beets, and finely shred the kale, then add it all to the bowl. Pick the pretty baby herb leaves into a cup of cold water, then finely chop the rest of the leaves and add to the bowl with the vinegar, 2 tablespoons of oil, and a pinch of sea salt and black pepper. Toss it all together well and divide between your serving bowls.

Preheat a grill pan to high. Halve, peel, and pit the avocados, then grill for 3 to 5 minutes, or until bar-marked. Meanwhile, trim the broccolini spears, blanch for 4 minutes in a pan of boiling water, then drain.

Place a grilled avocado half on top of each salad, fill each avo well with cottage cheese, then pile the broccolini on top. Spoon over the harissa and scatter over the seeds. Hold the pomegranate half cut-side down in your fingers, bash the back of it with a spoon so all the seeds tumble out over the salads, then serve. This is delicious pimped with a few slices of poached chicken (see page 230) or salmon, or with a little sprinkling of crumbled feta cheese.

Seasonal swap in

When beautiful baby beets are in season, pick up a mixed-color bunch, scrub them clean, parboil, then peel, quarter, and roast them until sticky, like we do in the restaurants.

CALORIES	FAT	SAT FAT	PROTEIN	CARBS	SUGAR	SALT	FIBER	3 PORTIONS
578kcal	29.1g	5.8g	22.9g	56.2g	13.5g	1g	12.9g	VEG & FRUIT

SHRIMP NOODLE SALAD
PASSION FRUIT DRESSING & SESAME SEEDS

Shrimp give us selenium, which our thyroid glands need to function properly and to keep our metabolic systems in check, meaning we can get everything we need from the food we eat

SERVES 4

30 MINUTES

12–16 large raw shell-on jumbo
   shrimp (1 lb)

7 oz fine rice noodles

3 passion fruit

1 tablespoon reduced-sodium
   soy sauce

1 teaspoon fish sauce

peanut oil

extra virgin olive oil

1 pinch of cayenne pepper

2 cloves of garlic

¾-inch piece of fresh gingerroot

2 limes

14 oz mixture of asparagus,
   scallions, carrots

3½ oz sprouts, such as chickpea
   sprouts, alfalfa sprouts

1 bunch of fresh mint (1 oz)

2 teaspoons raw sesame seeds

4 tablespoons plain yogurt

Pull the middle part of each shrimp shell off, leaving the head and tail intact, then run a small sharp knife down the back and remove the vein (or you could ask your fishmonger to do this for you). In a bowl, cover the noodles with boiling kettle water to rehydrate them.

Halve the passion fruit and scrape the seeds into a large bowl. Add the soy and fish sauces, 1 tablespoon each of peanut and extra virgin olive oil, and the cayenne. Crush in the unpeeled garlic through a garlic crusher. Peel and grate in the ginger, squeeze in all the lime juice, and mix well. Spoon 2 tablespoons of the dressing over the shrimp, toss and leave to marinate.

Prep your veg—trim the woody ends off the asparagus, trim the scallions, then finely slice both, and peel and matchstick the carrots. Toss it all in the remaining dressing with the sprouts. Pick, slice, and add the mint leaves, drain and add the noodles, then toss together well.

Place the marinated shrimp in a large non-stick frying pan on a medium-high heat in a single layer. Cook for 6 minutes, turning halfway and sprinkling in the sesame seeds when you turn them. Serve the gnarly shrimp with the noodle salad, scraping over the sticky sesame seeds from the bottom of the pan, and enjoy it all with a dollop of yogurt on the side.

CALORIES	FAT	SAT FAT	PROTEIN	CARBS	SUGAR	SALT	FIBER	2 PORTIONS VEG & FRUIT
367kcal	9.5g	2g	21.1g	48g	5.7g	0.9g	2.9	

MOORISH CRUNCH SALAD
COUSCOUS PARCELS, ORANGE, & HARISSA

The bonus of using three lovely oranges here means that this beautifully bright salad provides us with our daily recommended intake of vitamin C, helping to keep our immune systems strong

SERVES 4

40 MINUTES

1 cup whole-wheat couscous

1 large or 2 small preserved
   lemons

5 oz small heirloom carrots

1 red onion

4 tablespoons white wine vinegar

½ a bunch of fresh mint (½ oz)

4 sheets of phyllo pastry (8¼ oz)

4 tablespoons plain yogurt

2 heaping tablespoons smooth
   peanut butter

1 lime

1 heaping teaspoon harissa

extra virgin olive oil

1½ oz shelled unsalted pistachios

3 oranges or blood oranges

1 Bibb lettuce

2 little gem lettuces or hearts
   of romaine

Preheat the oven to 350°F. Place the couscous in a bowl. Finely chop and add the preserved lemon(s), removing any seeds, then just cover with boiling kettle water, pop a plate on top, and leave to fluff up. Wash the carrots and quarter lengthways. Peel, halve, and finely slice the onion. Toss both in a shallow bowl with the vinegar and a good pinch of sea salt to draw out excess moisture (you'll drain the liquor off, so don't worry about the amount of salt).

Pick and finely chop most of the mint leaves and stir through the couscous, fluffing it up with a fork, then season to perfection. Unroll the phyllo pastry and spoon one-quarter of the couscous onto the middle of one sheet. Flatten into a square, then fold the phyllo up around it, creating a square parcel. Repeat with the remaining couscous and phyllo, then place the parcels on a baking sheet and bake for 20 minutes, or until lightly golden and crisp—this is a cute way to serve couscous and adds epic texture to the salad. In a bowl, mix the yogurt, peanut butter, 2 teaspoons of preserved lemon liquor from the jar, and the lime juice, loosening with a splash of water, if needed. Loosen the harissa with 1 tablespoon of oil in a little bowl. Crush the pistachios in a pestle and mortar. Peel the oranges and cut into thin rounds. Wash the lettuces, trim the bases, then cut the Bibb lettuce into quarters and the little gems in half.

Now the fun bit: to serve, divide the lettuce between your plates and drizzle over the peanutty yogurt dressing. Drain and divide up the pickled carrots and onions, then tear each phyllo parcel in half and add to the plates with a few orange slices. Drizzle the parcels with harissa oil, scatter with pistachios, pick over the remaining mint leaves, then mix it all up and tuck in!

CALORIES	FAT	SAT FAT	PROTEIN	CARBS	SUGAR	SALT	FIBER	2 PORTIONS VEG & FRUIT
573kcal	20.6g	4.2g	19.3g	78.6g	25.4g	1.4g	9.9g	

CHOPPED CHARRED VEG SALAD
COUSCOUS, WRAPS, FETA, MINT, NUTS, & SEEDS

— Although feta cheese is a high-fat ingredient, using it in small amounts like I've done here —
can be healthy, giving us a source of chloride, which in turn helps us digest the food we eat

SERVES 4

1 HOUR

1¾ oz blanched hazelnuts

1 oz raw sunflower and sesame seeds

½ teaspoon each fennel seeds, cumin seeds, dried red chili flakes, dried oregano

2 mixed-color zucchini

2 mixed-color peppers

2 ripe beefsteak tomatoes

2 red onions

1 large eggplant

⅓ cup whole-wheat couscous

1 lemon

1 tablespoon cider vinegar

extra virgin olive oil

1 bunch of fresh mint (1 oz)

4 whole-wheat tortilla wraps

4 tablespoons Greek yogurt

1¾ oz feta cheese

Start by toasting the nuts, all the seeds, the chili flakes, and oregano in your widest pan on a medium-high heat until smelling fantastic. Tip into a pestle and mortar and roughly crush, returning the empty pan to the heat. Put the whole zucchini, peppers, tomatoes, peeled onions, and eggplant into the dry pan (use two pans, if you need to). Blacken and char all over, turning regularly and removing to a large bowl as each veg is done. Meanwhile, put the couscous into a bowl and finely grate over the lemon zest. Just cover with boiling kettle water, then pop a plate on top and leave to fluff up.

Once cool enough to handle, pull off any large bits of blackened veg skin that come away easily, but don't stress too much about getting it all. Seed the peppers, then chop all the veg into bite-sized chunks, returning to the bowl as you go, along with any lovely juices. Dress with the lemon juice, vinegar, 2 tablespoons of oil, and a pinch of sea salt and black pepper. Pick, finely chop, and add the mint leaves (saving the pretty ones for garnish), then toss well.

Warm the tortilla wraps in a dry frying pan for just 30 seconds. Pour a little of the veg dressing over the couscous, fluff up, and divide between your plates with the veg, yogurt, crumbled feta, the nut mixture, and reserved mint leaves. Delicious with a drizzle of chili sauce.

---- *Get outside* ----

In the warmer months, seize the opportunity to cook your veg on the barbecue to give extra smokiness and flavor—delicious!

CALORIES	FAT	SAT FAT	PROTEIN	CARBS	SUGAR	SALT	FIBER	4 PORTIONS VEG & FRUIT
568kcal	25.3g	6g	20.7g	64.2g	17.4g	1.5g	20.7g	

SUPER BRUSSELS SPROUTS SLAW
CITRUS, FLAKED SALMON, FETA, & NUTS

— Brilliant Brussels sprouts are super-high in vitamin C, which we need, along with the mineral —
phosphorus found in salmon and couscous, to keep our bones strong and healthy

SERVES 4

25 MINUTES

2 cups whole-wheat couscous

2 oranges

1 lemon

¾ oz blanched hazelnuts

1 x 17-oz piece of salmon fillet,
   skin on, scaled, pin-boned

7 oz Brussels sprouts

3½ oz purple kale

5 oz small carrots

2 large eating apples

1 bunch of scallions

4 tablespoons plain yogurt

1 tablespoon whole-grain mustard

¾ oz feta cheese

Place the couscous in a bowl and use a vegetable peeler to top it with strips of zest from both oranges and the lemon. Just cover with boiling kettle water, pop a plate on top, and leave to fluff up. Toast the hazelnuts in a small dry frying pan on a medium heat until golden, then lightly crush in a pestle and mortar and put aside until needed. Return the pan to a medium heat. Place the salmon skin-side up in the dry pan for 8 minutes, turning halfway. When it's just cooked through, remove from the pan. Gently pull off the skin and return to the pan to fry until nice and crispy.

Meanwhile, pull off any tatty outer leaves from the Brussels sprouts. Trim the tough stalks away from the kale, then wash with the carrots and apples. Trim the scallions. Push it all through the fine slicing attachment of a food processor, decanting into a large bowl as you go. Squeeze over the lemon juice and the juice from 1 orange, add the yogurt and mustard, then mix and scrunch together with clean hands, taste, and season to perfection.

Remove the citrus peel from the top of the couscous, fluff up the couscous with a fork, and divide between your plates. Portion up the slaw, crumble over the feta, sprinkle with the toasted hazelnuts, then flake over the salmon and crack over the crispy skin. Serve with orange wedges, for squeezing over.

CALORIES	FAT	SAT FAT	PROTEIN	CARBS	SUGAR	SALT	FIBER	2 PORTIONS
598kcal	20.4g	4g	38.8g	68.7g	15.8g	0.6g	9.3g	VEG & FRUIT

KOREAN BIBIMBAP BOWL
RICE, VEG, PORK, & HOT CHILI SAUCE

___ Using tenderloin, which is a leaner cut of pork, means we don't consume too much saturated ___
fat, and we get a good dose of the B-vitamin thiamin, which our hearts need to function

SERVES 4

1 HOUR

2 tablespoons raw sesame seeds

1½ cups brown rice

1 teabag of mint green tea

4 large eggs

2½ lbs mixed crunchy veg, such
   as carrots, Napa cabbage,
   baby corn, sugar snap peas,
   beansprouts

10-oz piece of pork tenderloin

½ an English cucumber

6 radishes

1 tablespoon rice wine vinegar

2 tablespoons hot chili sauce

1 teaspoon reduced-sodium
   soy sauce

1 lime

1¾ oz baby spinach

1 cup sprouting cress

Toast the sesame seeds in a large deep pan until lightly golden, then tip into a small dish. Return the pan to the heat. Pour in the rice, add the teabag and a pinch of sea salt, then cover with 16 cups of water and cook according to the rice package timings. When the water comes to a boil, rinse the eggs, then carefully lower them in to soft-boil for 5½ minutes, or until cooked to your liking. Remove the eggs and place a sieve in the pan so it sits in the water. Peel the carrots into ribbons and shred the Napa cabbage. Veg by veg, quickly blanch each crunchy veg in the sieve for just a minute or two while the rice carries on cooking, shaking off any excess water and arranging in piles on a platter as you go. Finely slice the pork tenderloin and toss in the sieve for 3 to 4 minutes, or until cooked through.

While the rice finishes off, scratch the fork down the outside of the cucumber, then finely slice into rounds. Halve the radishes and toss both with the vinegar and a pinch of salt in a bowl. In a separate bowl, mix the chili and soy sauces with the lime zest and half the juice. Cut the remaining lime half into four wedges, pile up the spinach, snip the cress, and peel the eggs. Once done, drain the rice, reserving the broth, which you can divide between four cups or glasses to serve on the side for an extra nutrient hit.

Serve the platter in the middle of the table, ready to divide up between bowls. The idea is to bust up your eggs and mix it all together before tucking in—it's a really fun way of celebrating different veg, condiments, flavors, and textures.

CALORIES	FAT	SAT FAT	PROTEIN	CARBS	SUGAR	SALT	FIBER	4 PORTIONS
572kcal	15.3g	3.8g	33.9g	79.4g	18.4g	0.7g	9.4g	VEG & FRUIT

SHRIMP & AVO COCKTAIL SALAD
BABY POTATOES, CRUNCHY VEG, & CRESS

My twist on a traditional shrimp cocktail uses plain yogurt—giving us lots of gut-friendly bacteria—and avocado to achieve a super-smooth, creamy sauce, as opposed to calorific mayo

SERVES 4

25 MINUTES

12 oz fresh or frozen peeled
cooked shrimp

1¾ lbs baby white potatoes

1 ripe avocado

6 heaping tablespoons plain
yogurt

2 lemons

½ a bunch of fresh basil (½ oz)

1 cucumber

4 scallions

½ an iceberg lettuce

7 oz ripe mixed-color cherry
tomatoes, on the vine

2 cups sprouting cress

extra virgin olive oil

7 oz fresh podded peas

1 fresh red chile

If using frozen shrimp, defrost overnight in the fridge or simply place in a bowl of cold water while you prep everything else, to save time.

Cook the baby potatoes in a large pan of boiling salted water for 15 to 20 minutes, or until cooked through, then drain and steam dry. Squash them into a large bowl and put aside. Meanwhile, peel and pit the avocado, putting the flesh into a blender with the yogurt and the juice of 1 lemon. Pick a small handful of baby basil leaves into a cup of cold water for later, then add the rest of the bunch to the blender and blitz it all until smooth. Taste and season to perfection, loosening with a splash of water, if needed.

Peel the cucumber, halve lengthways, scrape out the watery core, and finely slice. Trim and finely slice the scallions. Halve and finely slice the iceberg. Quarter the cherry tomatoes. Snip the cress. Add it all to the bowl of potatoes and dress with 1 tablespoon of oil and the juice of the remaining lemon. Taste, season to perfection, and divide between your plates.

Drain the shrimp well, if needed, then toss with 2 tablespoons of the sauce and the fresh peas, to coat. Portion them up, spooning the remaining sauce elegantly on top. Finely slice and scatter over the chile, to taste, then tuck in.

CALORIES	FAT	SAT FAT	PROTEIN	CARBS	SUGAR	SALT	FIBER	3 PORTIONS
373kcal	10.6g	3.6g	23.8g	48.1g	13.1g	1.5g	7.4g	VEG & FRUIT

WARM SMOKED TROUT SALAD
BABY POTATOES, BEETS, & SOFT-BOILED EGGS

— Trout is a brilliant source of protein, which we need to repair and build our muscles. It also —
gives us vitamin D, helping our muscles to function and making this a great post-gym salad

SERVES 4

25 MINUTES

1¾ lbs baby white potatoes

4 large eggs

7 oz fine green beans

1 bunch of asparagus (12 oz)

6 heaping tablespoons plain
  yogurt

2 tablespoons white wine vinegar

3 teaspoons jarred grated
  horseradish

1 bunch of fresh chives (1 oz)

1 lemon

4 x 2½-oz smoked trout fillets

3½ oz raw mixed-color baby
  beets

To save time and washing up, as the potatoes cook we're going to utilize their cooking water to maximum effect, so timing is important. Wash the potatoes, halve any larger ones, then cook in a large pan with plenty of boiling salted water for 15 to 20 minutes, or until cooked through. Rinse the eggs, then at the same time, soft-boil in the potato water for 5½ minutes, removing to a bowl of cold water (you can cook them for longer, if you prefer). Trim just the stalk ends off the green beans and add for the last 7 minutes, and trim the woody ends off the asparagus, adding for the last 3 minutes.

Meanwhile, for the dressing, mix the yogurt, vinegar, and horseradish together in a bowl. Finely chop the chives, add most of them, mix well, add a nice squeeze of lemon juice, then taste and season to perfection.

Drain the potatoes and green veg and leave to steam dry for a few minutes. Cut the potatoes into bite-sized chunks, slice up the green beans and asparagus, and toss it all in the dressing, then pour over a large platter or divide between your plates. Flake over the smoked trout, then peel and finely slice the beets, ideally on a mandolin (use the guard!) or using a vegetable peeler, and sprinkle over the top. Peel and halve the eggs and dot around, then scatter over the reserved chives and squeeze over any remaining lemon juice.

CALORIES	FAT	SAT FAT	PROTEIN	CARBS	SUGAR	SALT	FIBER	2 PORTIONS
386kcal	12.3g	3.4g	30.9g	40.4g	10g	1.3g	5.8g	VEG & FRUIT

SUPER SALAD PLATTER
AVO, SWEET POTATOES, BROCCOLI, & BEETS

Both quinoa and cashew nuts are high in the mineral copper, which our bodies need for everything from immune and nervous system function to efficiently transporting iron around

SERVES 4

1 HOUR 20 MINUTES

1 teaspoon cumin seeds

2 small sweet potatoes
   (7 oz each)

12 oz broccoli

olive oil

1 oz unsalted cashew nuts

1 oz mixed raw pumpkin,
   sunflower, and sesame seeds

8 oz vac-packed or freshly
   cooked beets

2 tablespoons balsamic vinegar

extra virgin olive oil

1½ cups quinoa

1 bunch of fresh mint (1 oz)

1 lemon

1 ripe avocado

6 tablespoons plain yogurt

1 cup sprouting cress

Preheat the oven to 350°F. Crush the cumin seeds in a pestle and mortar, then rub onto the washed sweet potatoes. Place in a roasting pan and cook in the oven for 30 minutes. Meanwhile, cut the woody end off the broccoli stalk, slice it, then chop the rest into large florets. Toss the broccoli into the sweet potato pan with 1 tablespoon of olive oil. Roast for another 30 minutes, or until the sweet potatoes are cooked through.

Toast the nuts and seeds in a dry frying pan on a medium heat until smelling fantastic, then crush in a pestle and mortar. Bash and mush up the beets as much as you can, then decant into a bowl with the balsamic and 1 tablespoon of extra virgin olive oil. Mix together, mashing with a fork, if needed. Cook the quinoa according to the package instructions, and drain well. Pick and finely chop the mint leaves (reserving the pretty ones for garnish) and stir through the quinoa with the finely grated lemon zest and the juice, then season to perfection.

Scatter the quinoa across a large platter. Once cool enough to handle, tear over chunks of roasted sweet potato and dot over the roasted broccoli. Halve the avocado and use a teaspoon to add curls of flesh to the platter. Dollop over the yogurt, spoon bombs of dressed beets on top, scatter over the toasted nuts and seeds and the reserved mint leaves, snip over the cress, and serve.

CALORIES	FAT	SAT FAT	PROTEIN	CARBS	SUGAR	SALT	FIBER	3 PORTIONS VEG & FRUIT
527kcal	19.8g	3.6g	18.5g	74.2g	21.8g	0.4g	10g	

SALMON CRUDO & CRISPBREADS
FENNEL, APPLE, FAVA BEANS, & AVOCADO

Brilliant fava beans are a source of several vitamins and minerals, including pantothenic acid, which both keeps our metabolic systems functioning and helps prevent us feeling tired

SERVES 4

20 MINUTES

1 x 14-oz piece of super-fresh
   salmon fillet, skin off, pin-boned

⅓ cup unsweetened apple juice

2 lemons

7 oz fava beans

1 bulb of fennel

1 ripe avocado

1 apple

1 teaspoon whole-grain mustard

extra virgin olive oil

optional: ½ a bunch of fresh
   dill (½ oz)

4 Swedish-style rye or
   whole-wheat crispbreads

4 heaping teaspoons cream cheese

Slice the salmon just under ½ inch thick, then lay the slices in a shallow dish and cover with the apple juice. Squeeze over the juice of half a lemon, add a pinch of sea salt, then leave aside—this will very subtly cure the fish.

Blanch the fava beans in a pan of boiling water for 2 minutes, then drain and pinch off the skins from any larger beans. Place all the beans in a large bowl. Quarter, finely slice, and add the fennel, picking and reserving any nice fennel tops. Peel and pit the avocado and slice into thin wedges, core the apple and slice into wedges the same size, then toss both into the bowl with the mustard, 1 tablespoon of oil, and the juice of 1 lemon. Mix well, then taste and season to perfection. Pick and scatter over the dill (if using), along with any reserved fennel tops.

Divide the salad and drained salmon between your plates, and serve with the crispbreads, cream cheese, and lemon wedges, for squeezing over.

Mix it up

You basically want a nice carb vehicle to enjoy on the side, so try crackers, rye bread, toast, or even a roll instead of crispbreads, if you prefer.

CALORIES	FAT	SAT FAT	PROTEIN	CARBS	SUGAR	SALT	FIBER	2 PORTIONS VEG & FRUIT
346kcal	18.7g	3.8g	26.8g	18.7g	8.6g	0.8g	6.8g	

CURRIES
& STEWS

Hearty, nutritious, delicious meals that

are sure to make everyone very happy

CHICKEN JALFREZI
BLACKENED PEPPERS & TOMATO RICE

The vitamin C from the peppers, chiles, and tomatoes helps us to absorb the iron
found in the beautiful spices in my homemade jalfrezi paste—double win!

SERVES 4

45 MINUTES

2 heaping tablespoons of jalfrezi
curry paste (see page 236)

3 heaping tablespoons plain
yogurt

4 x 4-oz boneless, skinless
chicken breasts

2 fresh green chiles

3 mixed-color peppers

2 tablespoons white wine vinegar

2 mixed-color onions

1½ cups basmati rice

1 x 14-oz can of plum tomatoes

cayenne pepper

½ a bunch of fresh cilantro
(½ oz)

1 lemon

Jarred Indian curry pastes are very good and convenient, but making your own is even better (see page 236). In a bowl, mix the paste with 1 heaping tablespoon of yogurt and a pinch of sea salt. Cut each chicken breast into four even-sized chunks and toss in the mixture, massaging well, then leave to marinate. In batches, prick then blacken the whole chiles and peppers over a direct flame on the stove, or in a grill pan on a high heat, until charred and blistered all over. Pop into a bowl, cover with plastic wrap for 10 minutes, then scrape off as much black skin as you can, discarding the stalks and seeds, and chop into 1½-inch chunks. Seed the chiles and lay in the vinegar on a small plate to lightly pickle.

Peel the onions, then cut into quarters and break apart into petals. Place a large casserole pan on a medium-high heat, scatter in the onions, and dry fry for 8 minutes, or until starting to char. Remove from the pan and use tongs to add the chicken in one layer, scraping up any excess marinade as you go. Fry for 2 minutes per side, or until golden, then return the onions to the pan with the chopped peppers and toss for 2 minutes to get the flavors going.

Put the rice into a pan of boiling salted water. Pour the canned tomatoes into a sieve over the rice so all the juice runs through, then cook according to the package instructions and drain. Tear the tomatoes into the chicken pan, add ⅔ cup of water, simmer for 10 to 15 minutes, or until the sauce is the consistency you like, then taste and season to perfection. Serve the curry and rice with the remaining yogurt, a pinch of cayenne, the picked cilantro leaves, and lemon wedges, with the pickled chiles on the side.

CALORIES	FAT	SAT FAT	PROTEIN	CARBS	SUGAR	SALT	FIBER	3 PORTIONS
504kcal	5.4g	1.5g	39g	80.1g	14.6g	0.9g	5.7g	VEG & FRUIT

SAG ALOO KORMA
SWEET POTATOES, CHARD, & CHICKPEAS

Brown rice is higher than white rice in lots of vitamins and minerals, including B-vitamins niacin and thiamin, which our nervous systems need to be able to function properly

SERVES 4

1 HOUR

1 lb potatoes

1 lb sweet potatoes

¾ cup brown basmati rice

olive oil

2 heaping tablespoons korma curry paste (see page 236)

1 bunch of scallions

1 lb mixed chard and spinach

1 x 15-oz can of chickpeas

1⅔ cups reduced-fat (2%) milk

1½ oz feta cheese

4 uncooked pappadams

1 lemon

Jarred Indian curry pastes are very good and convenient, but making your own is even better (see page 236). Wash the potatoes and sweet potatoes (leaving the skins on for extra nutritional benefit), chop into 1¼-inch chunks, then cook in a large pan of boiling salted water for 15 minutes, or until cooked through. Drain and leave to steam dry for 2 minutes.

Cook the rice in a pan of boiling salted water according to the package instructions. Put a large, wide non-stick pan on a medium heat with 1 tablespoon of oil and the curry paste. Add all the dry potatoes and cook for 10 minutes, stirring occasionally and letting the potatoes catch and go dark golden (this is where you make your investment in flavor and texture). Trim, slice, and add the scallions. Finely slice the chard stalks, roughly slice the leaves, then, in batches, stir into the pan with the spinach, to wilt. Pour in the chickpeas (juice and all), the milk, and 6 tablespoons of water. Simmer for 15 minutes, or until thick and delicious, stirring occasionally. Taste, season to perfection, then crumble over the feta.

Just before serving, one by one puff up your dry pappadams in the microwave for around 30 seconds each. Drain and divide up the rice, portion up the korma, and serve with the pappadams and lemon wedges, for squeezing over.

CALORIES	FAT	SAT FAT	PROTEIN	CARBS	SUGAR	SALT	FIBER	3 PORTIONS VEG & FRUIT
600kcal	14.9g	4.8g	21.7g	101.2g	16.5g	1.5g	11.1g	

THAI GREEN CHICKEN CURRY
EGGPLANT, BABY CORN, CASHEWS, & LIME

Using flavor-packed chicken breasts here provides us with plenty of B vitamins, which our bodies use for lots of things, such as making red blood cells, keeping us awake and alert

SERVES 6

45 MINUTES

1 large eggplant

2 tablespoons unsalted cashew nuts

2 teaspoons raw sesame seeds

3 heaping tablespoons Thai green curry paste (see page 236)

1 x 14-oz can of light coconut milk

2 red onions

6 oz baby corn

4 x 4-oz boneless, skinless chicken breasts

1⅔ cups reduced-fat (2%) milk

13 oz whole-wheat noodles

2 teaspoons sesame oil

4 sprigs of fresh basil

1 lime

Put a grill pan on a high heat. Quarter the eggplant lengthways, cut into 1¼-inch chunks, and in batches start to char it in the grill pan. Put a large wok or pan on a medium-high heat alongside it, quickly toast the cashew nuts, followed by the sesame seeds, until golden, then tip into a pestle and mortar and lightly crush. Put the Thai green curry paste into the wok, followed by the coconut milk. Transfer the charred eggplant to the wok as it's done. Peel and quarter the onions, then break them apart into petals and grill, along with the baby corn, adding it all to the sauce once nicely charred.

Finely slice the chicken breasts and stir into the sauce with the milk. Simmer it all for 8 minutes, or until the chicken is cooked through, stirring occasionally. Taste and season to perfection. Meanwhile, cook the noodles according to the package instructions, then drain, toss with the sesame oil, and divide between your bowls.

Serve the curry sprinkled with the crushed nuts and seeds, and the picked basil leaves. Add a squeeze of lime juice, to taste, and enjoy.

CALORIES	FAT	SAT FAT	PROTEIN	CARBS	SUGAR	SALT	FIBER	2 PORTIONS VEG & FRUIT
512kcal	13.3g	6g	33.2g	64.3g	11.5g	0.7g	4.4g	

VEGGIE GURKHA CURRY
EGGPLANT, SWEET POTATOES, & CHICKPEAS

Using yogurt here instead of coconut milk reduces the fat content, while also giving us an extra hit of both calcium and phosphorus, the minerals that make up our bones and teeth

SERVES 6
1 HOUR 45 MINUTES
PLUS MARINATING

1½-inch piece of fresh gingerroot

4 cloves of garlic

1–2 fresh red chiles

4 cardamom pods

4 cloves

1 heaping teaspoon each of fennel seeds, cumin seeds, ground turmeric, ground cinnamon

4 fresh bay leaves

1 bunch of fresh cilantro (1 oz)

2 cups plain yogurt

2 large onions

2 large eggplants

2 sweet potatoes (10 oz each)

1 x 14-oz can of plum tomatoes

1 x 19-oz can of chickpeas

2¼ cups brown basmati rice

Peel the ginger and garlic, seed the chiles, and place in a food processor. Crush the cardamom pods, and add just the inner seeds to the processor, along with the cloves, fennel and cumin seeds, turmeric, and cinnamon. Tear the stalks out of the bay, adding the leaves to the processor. Pick the nice cilantro leaves into a cup of cold water for later, then add the rest of the bunch to the processor with 1 cup of yogurt and a pinch of sea salt and black pepper, and blitz until smooth. Peel and quarter the onions. Wash the eggplants and sweet potatoes, then chop into 1¼-inch chunks. Toss the veg and marinade in a large roasting pan (16 x 12 inches) and, if you can, leave for 1 hour, or even overnight, to let those flavors start penetrating the veg.

Preheat the oven to 350°F. Roast the pan of veg for 1 hour, or until dark golden and cooked through. Transfer the pan to a medium heat on the stove, then pour in the tomatoes, breaking them up with a wooden spoon as you go, along with 1½ cans' worth of water. Stir in the chickpeas (juice and all). Leave to bubble and simmer away for 20 minutes, then taste and season to perfection. Meanwhile, cook the rice in a large pan of boiling salted water according to the package instructions, then drain and return to the pan over a low heat so it gets a bit gnarly at the edges.

Portion up the rice. Ripple the remaining yogurt through the curry, then serve sprinkled with the reserved cilantro leaves.

CALORIES	FAT	SAT FAT	PROTEIN	CARBS	SUGAR	SALT	FIBER	4 PORTIONS VEG & FRUIT
572kcal	9g	3.4g	18.7g	111.6g	22.4g	0.6g	7.4g	

AFRICAN SHRIMP CURRY
SCOTCH BONNETS & STICKY OKRA BASMATI

Adding lovely base flavor here, peanut butter is high in the B-vitamin biotin, which we need
in order for our nervous systems to function properly, and for strong, healthy, luscious locks

SERVES 4

45 MINUTES

1 lb large raw peeled shrimp

2 mixed-color peppers

2 red onions

2 fresh Scotch bonnet chiles

2 tablespoons red wine vinegar

olive oil

2 teaspoons ground coriander

2 teaspoons sweet smoked
  paprika

1¼ lbs ripe tomatoes

2 cups chicken or veg stock

1 tablespoon peanut butter

1½ cups basmati rice

6 oz okra

4 tablespoons plain yogurt

Use a small sharp knife to lightly score down the back of the shrimp (and remove the vein, if needed). Seed the peppers, peel the onions, and chop into chunks about the same thickness as the shrimp. Carefully seed and finely chop the Scotch bonnet chiles (wear gloves, if you want). Place the peppers, onions, and chiles in a large bowl. In a smaller bowl, mix together the vinegar, 1 tablespoon of oil, a pinch of sea salt, the ground coriander, and paprika. Pour half the mixture over the veg and toss well, tossing the shrimp into the smaller bowl.

Put a large non-stick pan on a medium-high heat. Cook the dressed veg for 10 minutes, stirring regularly. Chop the tomatoes into ¾-inch dice and stir into the pan. Pour in the stock, add the peanut butter, and simmer for 10 minutes. Add the shrimp for another 4 minutes, then taste and season to perfection.

While the curry is simmering, cook the rice in a large pan with plenty of boiling salted water according to the package instructions. Trim and finely slice the okra and add to the rice pan for the last 4 minutes, which will naturally make the rice super-sticky and comforting. Drain well, then serve up with the curry, topping each portion with a dollop of cooling yogurt.

CALORIES	FAT	SAT FAT	PROTEIN	CARBS	SUGAR	SALT	FIBER	3 PORTIONS VEG & FRUIT
552kcal	9.9g	2.4g	37.8g	9.9g	2.4g	0.9g	6.1g	

BAKED TARKA DAAL
CAULIFLOWER, SPLIT PEAS, & CHAPATTIS

__ Yellow split peas are the secret of incredible comforting texture here—packed with protein and __
fiber, they also give us a hit of the B-vitamin thiamin, so our hearts can function properly

SERVES 8
1 HOUR 45 MINUTES

6 cloves of garlic

1½-inch piece of fresh gingerroot

2 fresh red chiles

olive oil

4 teaspoons black mustard seeds

1 cinnamon stick

2 onions

1 head of cauliflower

2 heaping teaspoons curry powder

1 ripe mango

6 cups veg stock

1 x 14-oz can of plum tomatoes

1 lb dried yellow split peas

8 whole-grain chapattis

8 tablespoons plain yogurt

1 bunch of fresh cilantro (1 oz)

Preheat the oven to 400°F. Peel and chop the garlic and ginger, then finely slice the chiles. Place it all in a large ovenproof casserole pan on a medium heat with 1 tablespoon of oil, the mustard seeds, and cinnamon stick. Let it get nicely golden, stirring regularly, while you peel the onions and chop them into ½-inch dice. Pull off and discard any tatty outer cauliflower leaves, then chop the inner leaves, stalk, and florets into rough ¾-inch chunks, removing the tough stalk end. Stir the onions, cauliflower, and curry powder into the pan and cook for 5 minutes, stirring regularly.

Cut the cheeks off the mango and peel them. Dice the flesh, then stir into the pan and cover with the stock. Add the tomatoes, breaking them up with a wooden spoon, then pour in 1½ cans' worth of water. Rinse and add the split peas. Boil for 10 minutes, then transfer to the oven for 40 minutes.

Pull out the pan, stir the daal well, then blitz half with an immersion blender (avoiding the cinnamon stick!) and stir back through to increase the comforting texture. Taste, season to perfection, loosening with a splash of water, if needed, then cook for 40 more minutes, or until thick and a satisfying crust has formed.

Just before serving, warm the chapattis in the oven for a couple of minutes. Serve each portion of daal with a good dollop of yogurt and sprinkled with picked cilantro leaves, with chapattis on the side, for dunking.

Freezer friendly
Batch up any extra portions, and freeze in labeled sandwich bags for a rainy day.

CALORIES	FAT	SAT FAT	PROTEIN	CARBS	SUGAR	SALT	FIBER	3 PORTIONS VEG & FRUIT
449kcal	11.2g	4g	20.4g	64.5g	11.9g	0.9g	11.2g	

CHINESE STEAK & TOFU STEW
STICKY RICE & BEANS, SZECHUAN SPRINKLE

— Adzuki beans pack a good nutritional punch, giving us a big hit of zinc, which we need in order to metabolize other vitamins and minerals, and to keep our bones strong and healthy —

SERVES 4

45 MINUTES

8 oz rump or sirloin steak

2 cloves of garlic

1½-inch piece of fresh gingerroot

1 fresh red chile

1 bunch of scallions

2 large carrots

8 oz mooli or radishes

1 heaping teaspoon Szechuan peppercorns

peanut oil

2 tablespoons Chinese chili bean paste (find it in Asian supermarkets)

4 cups veg stock

1 x 15-oz can of adzuki beans

1¼ cups pudding or risotto rice

1 tablespoon cornstarch

7 oz broccolini

12 oz firm silken tofu

Get your prep done first, for smooth cooking. Chop the steak into ½-inch chunks, trimming away and discarding any fat. Peel and finely chop the garlic and ginger and slice the chile. Trim the scallions, finely slice the top green halves and put aside, then chop the whites into ¾-inch chunks. Peel the carrots and mooli or radishes, and chop to a similar size. Place a large pan on a medium-high heat and toast the Szechuan peppercorns while it heats up. Tip into a pestle and mortar, leaving the pan on the heat. Place the chopped steak in the pan with 1 tablespoon of peanut oil. Stir until starting to brown, then add the garlic, ginger, chile, the white scallions, carrots, and mooli or radishes. Cook for 5 minutes, stirring regularly, then stir in the chili bean paste for 30 seconds until dark. Pour in the stock and simmer for 10 minutes.

Meanwhile, drain the beans, put them into a pan with the rice and a pinch of sea salt, and cover by ½ inch with cold water. Place on a high heat, bring to a boil, then simmer until the water level meets the rice. Cover and leave on the lowest heat for 12 minutes, or until cooked through, stirring occasionally.

Taste the stew and season to perfection. Mix the cornstarch with 2 table-spoons of cold water until combined, then stir into the stew. Trim and stir in the broccolini. Chop the tofu into ¾-inch chunks and drop them in, then pop a lid on and keep on a low heat for 5 to 8 minutes while the stew thickens up and the broccolini just cooks through. Serve the stew scattered with the sliced green scallions, with the sticky rice and beans on the side. Finely crush and scatter over some Szechuan pepper. Nice with drips of chili oil, to taste.

CALORIES	FAT	SAT FAT	PROTEIN	CARBS	SUGAR	SALT	FIBER	2 PORTIONS VEG & FRUIT
561kcal	13.3g	2.9g	36.2g	77.8g	8.4g	0.7g	6.1g	

CHICKEN KORMA
CAULIFLOWER & BROWN RICE

— Bulking up the rice with an extra veg portion here, as we've done with cauliflower, means we also get a hit of vitamins C and K, which we need for strong and healthy bones —

SERVES 4

1 HOUR 10 MINUTES

2 teaspoons black mustard seeds

2 onions

olive oil

2 heaping tablespoons korma curry paste (see page 236)

4 chicken thighs, skin on, bone in

14 oz small heirloom or baby carrots

2½-inch piece of fresh gingerroot

3 fresh red chiles

¾ cup brown basmati rice

½ a small cauliflower (12 oz)

1 cup reduced-fat (2%) milk

1 cup plain yogurt

½ a bunch of fresh cilantro (½ oz)

Jarred Indian curry pastes are very good and convenient, but making your own is even better (see page 236). Preheat the oven to 350°F. Put the mustard seeds into a wide ovenproof pan on a medium-high heat. Leave them to pop while you peel and quarter the onions, then add to the pan with 1 tablespoon of oil and the curry paste. Pull the skin off the chicken and discard, then stir the thighs into the pan. Cook for 8 minutes, turning the chicken and onion wedges occasionally with tongs. Meanwhile, wash the carrots, and peel and finely slice the ginger. Stir into the pan with the whole chiles, then transfer to the oven for 35 minutes.

After 20 minutes, cook the rice in a large pan of boiling salted water according to the package instructions. Pull off and discard any tatty outer cauliflower leaves, then chop the inner leaves, stalk, and florets into small chunks, removing the tough stalk end. Add all the cauliflower to the rice for the last 10 minutes, to cook through, then drain.

Transfer the chicken pan to a low heat on the stove, pour in the milk, and simmer for 10 minutes, then remove and stand for a couple of minutes to prevent it from splitting. Blob the yogurt in and around, gently shake to allow it to marble and mix in, then taste and season to perfection. Serve with the cauliflower rice, sprinkled with a few fresh cilantro leaves. Chop and stir through some of the soft charred chile for extra heat, if you like.

CALORIES	FAT	SAT FAT	PROTEIN	CARBS	SUGAR	SALT	FIBER	3 PORTIONS VEG & FRUIT
500kcal	20g	6g	28.6g	56.6g	22.6g	0.7g	7.4g	

SPRING CHICKEN STEW
LOADSA LOVELY VEG, BACON, & BARLEY

Humble pearl barley—a brilliant pantry staple—is a source of several essential vitamins
and minerals, especially manganese, which we need for good bone health

SERVES 4

1 HOUR 10 MINUTES

olive oil

2 rashers of smoked bacon

2 sprigs of fresh rosemary

2 onions

2 carrots

14 oz white potatoes

½ cup pearl barley

1 heaping tablespoon all-purpose
  whole-grain flour

2 cups chicken stock

2 cups reduced-fat (2%) milk

2 zucchini

1 bunch of asparagus (12 oz)

7 oz green beans

4 x 4-oz boneless, skinless
  chicken breasts

1 tablespoon mint sauce

Put a large casserole pan on a medium heat with 1 tablespoon of oil. Finely slice and add the bacon, strip in the rosemary leaves, and leave to get golden, stirring regularly. Meanwhile, start prepping your veg. The idea here is to chop everything roughly the same size—around ¾ inch—stirring each veg into the pan as you prep it. Peel, chop, and add the onions, followed by the carrots, then the potatoes. Stir in the pearl barley and cook everything for 10 minutes, or until starting to soften but not color, stirring regularly.

Stir in the flour, followed gradually by the stock and the milk. Simmer for 10 minutes, while you trim and quarter the zucchini lengthways, trim the woody ends off the asparagus, trim just the stalk end off the beans, then chop it all into ¾-inch chunks. Chop the chicken into ¾-inch chunks, too. Stir the chicken and zucchini into the pan, cover with a scrunched sheet of wet parchment paper, and simmer on a low heat for 20 minutes. Give it a good stir, add the asparagus and beans, replace the paper and cook for a further 20 minutes, or until thickened and cooked through, stirring occasionally. Stir the mint sauce through the stew, taste, season to perfection, and serve.

CALORIES	FAT	SAT FAT	PROTEIN	CARBS	SUGAR	SALT	FIBER	4 PORTIONS
549kcal	12.5g	3.6g	48.2g	64.8g	20.5g	0.8g	7.2g	VEG & FRUIT

BALINESE CHICKEN CURRY
PURPLE KALE RICE, CHILE, & LEMONGRASS

As well as adding a vibrant splash of color to the rice in this recipe, super-nutritious purple kale is high in folic acid, a B vitamin our bodies need for efficient immune function

SERVES 6

1 HOUR

1¼ inch piece of fresh gingerroot

4 cloves of garlic

1 bunch of scallions

2 fresh red chiles

1½ oz unsalted cashew nuts

4 kaffir lime leaves

1 teaspoon ground turmeric

2 teaspoons fish sauce

10 oz oyster mushrooms

1 ripe mango

3 x 7-oz boneless, skinless
   chicken breasts

olive oil

1 lb fine green beans

2 limes

1 x 14-oz can of light coconut milk

2¼ cups basmati rice

8 oz purple kale

2 stalks of lemongrass

Peel the ginger and garlic, trim the scallions, halve and seed 1 chile, then char and soften it all in a large casserole pan on a medium-high heat with the cashews until everything is just starting to catch, tossing often. Tip into a blender with the lime leaves, turmeric, fish sauce, 1 teaspoon of black pepper, and a pinch of sea salt, and blitz into a paste.

Return the pan to a medium heat and dry char the mushrooms for 5 minutes so they get dark golden and nutty. Cut the cheeks off the mango and peel, then cut both the mango and chicken breasts into ½-inch slices. Remove the mushrooms to a plate, then add 1 tablespoon of oil and the paste to the pan. Stir and fry for 1 minute to get the flavors going, then add the chicken and mango and stir-fry for 5 minutes. Halve the green beans and add to the pan, returning the mushrooms, too. Squeeze in the juice of 1 lime, pour in the coconut milk, swirl a splash of water around the empty can, and pour into the pan. Bring to a boil, then simmer for 10 minutes, or until slightly thickened, stirring occasionally. Taste and season to perfection. Meanwhile, cook the rice in a large pan of boiling salted water according to the package instructions. Pull the kale leaves off the stalks, tear into small pieces, and chuck into the rice pan after 5 minutes, to cook through and add color.

Whack the stalks of lemongrass on your work surface to crush them, then remove the tough outer layer. Halve and seed the remaining chile and chop super-finely with the lemongrass. Drain the rice and serve with the curry, with a sprinkle of lemongrass and chile, to your taste, and with lime wedges on the side, for squeezing over.

CALORIES	FAT	SAT FAT	PROTEIN	CARBS	SUGAR	SALT	FIBER	2 PORTIONS VEG & FRUIT
551kcal	13.7g	5.4g	36.6g	74.9g	9g	0.8g	3.4g	

BEEF & GUINNESS STEW
ENGLISH MUSTARD PEARL BARLEY

The benefit of skirt steak is that it's leaner than many other cuts of beef, plus it's high in the mineral zinc, which we need to keep our hair, skin, and nails nice and healthy—triple win!

SERVES 6
2 HOURS 30 MINUTES

2¼ cups pearl barley

olive oil

3½ oz baby silverskin pickled onions

1 large onion

3 large carrots

1 celery heart

½ a bunch of fresh thyme (½ oz)

1¾ lbs rutabaga

¾ oz dried porcini mushrooms

1 lb beef skirt steak

4 cups beef or chicken stock

½ x 440-ml can of Guinness

1 lb fresh seasonal greens, such as kale, cabbage, chard

¾ oz Cheddar cheese

4 heaping teaspoons English mustard

Preheat the oven to 350°F. In a large pan, cover the pearl barley with plenty of cold water and leave to soak. Put a large casserole pan on a medium-high heat with 1 tablespoon of oil and the whole pickled onions. Peel and quarter the regular onion, then pull the quarters apart into petals and add to the pan. Stir regularly while you wash and trim the carrots and celery and slice both ¼ inch thick at an angle. Stir them into the pan, then strip in the thyme leaves. Cook and stir for 10 minutes while you peel the rutabaga and chop it into 1¼-inch chunks, and finely chop the dried porcini. Stir both into the pan, then slice the beef 1¼ inch thick and add that, too. After a couple of minutes, pour in the stock and Guinness. Bring up to a simmer, cover with a scrunched sheet of wet parchment paper, and cook in the oven for 1 hour.

Remove the parchment, then cook the stew for another hour, or until the meat is tender. Drain the pearl barley and re-cover with boiling water, then cook according to the package instructions. Pick through your greens, discarding any tough stalks, and steam in a colander or sieve above the pearl barley for the last 10 minutes. Reserving a little cooking water, drain the pearl barley and return it to the pan, grate over the cheese, add the English mustard and a splash of the reserved water, and mix together.

Taste the stew and season to perfection, then serve up with the mustard pearl barley and the freshly steamed greens on the side.

CALORIES	FAT	SAT FAT	PROTEIN	CARBS	SUGAR	SALT	FIBER	3 PORTIONS VEG & FRUIT
576kcal	9.9g	2.3g	39.8g	82.3g	16.3g	1.5g	6.1g	

TRAYBAKES

Let the oven do all the hard work
with these clever assembly-job meals

CHICKEN & CHORIZO BAKE
PEPPERS, SWEET POTATOES, & SPUDS

Both types of potatoes plus peppers mean this dish is jam-packed with vitamin C, a nutrient our bodies use for everything from keeping our teeth and skin healthy to protecting our cells

SERVES 4

1 HOUR 10 MINUTES

2½ oz quality chorizo

2 cloves of garlic

1 chicken bouillon cube

1 sprig of fresh rosemary

2 tablespoons sherry vinegar

4 chicken thighs, skin on, bone in

2 small sweet potatoes
(7 oz each)

2 baking potatoes (1 lb)

2 red onions

2 mixed-color peppers

1 bunch of fresh Italian parsley
(1 oz)

4 tablespoons plain yogurt

cayenne pepper

1 fresh red chile

2 tablespoons whole almonds

1 lemon

Preheat the oven to 400°F. Chop the chorizo, peel the garlic, and place both in a blender. Crumble in the bouillon cube, strip in the rosemary leaves, add the vinegar, then cover with 1¼ cups of boiling water. Put the lid on securely, cover with a kitchen towel, and, holding it in place, blitz until smooth.

Pull the skin off the chicken and discard, then place the thighs in a large roasting pan (16 x 12 inches). Wash all the potatoes (leaving the skins on for extra nutritional benefit) and chop into 1½-inch chunks. Peel the onions, seed the peppers, chop them into 1½-inch chunks too, and add all the veg to the pan. Pick over half the parsley leaves, then pour over the chorizo broth and mix it all together. Cover tightly with aluminum foil, place over the stove on a high heat for 2 minutes, then pop into the oven. Bake for 30 minutes, then remove the foil, pull the chicken up to the top to get golden, and cook for another 30 minutes, or until bubbling and the chicken and veg are cooked through.

Meanwhile, pick the rest of the parsley leaves onto a plate. Spoon the yogurt alongside and add a few pinches of cayenne next to it. Finely slice the chile and almonds and add to the plate, then finely grate over the lemon zest. When the traybake is ready, serve with the plate of garnishes alongside, letting everyone help themselves to yogurt and sprinkles.

CALORIES	FAT	SAT FAT	PROTEIN	CARBS	SUGAR	SALT	FIBER	3 PORTIONS VEG & FRUIT
432kcal	16g	4.6g	25.8g	49.6g	12g	1.5g	6.4g	

MANGO TERIYAKI SALMON
BROWN RICE & CHILE CUCUMBER PICKLE

___ I've used mighty mango here instead of sugar to create that wonderful sweetness we associate ___
with teriyaki sauce, plus it gives us a nice hit of vitamin C, helping us to think properly

SERVES 4

50 MINUTES

1⅙ cups brown rice

peanut oil

1 ripe mango

4 cloves of garlic

1½-inch piece of fresh gingerroot

3 limes

2 tablespoons reduced-sodium
   soy sauce

½ an English cucumber

1 fresh red chile

4 tablespoons white wine vinegar

4 x 4-oz salmon fillets, skin on,
   scaled, pin-boned

1 bunch of scallions

8 oz broccoli

½ a bunch of fresh mint (½ oz)

2 teaspoons raw sesame seeds

4 tablespoons plain yogurt

Cook the rice in a large pan of boiling salted water according to the package instructions, then drain. Rub a roasting pan (12 x 10 inches) with 1 teaspoon of peanut oil, then add the rice in an even layer. Meanwhile, wash the mango, cut the cheeks off the pit, peel, and put the flesh into a blender, reserving the skin. Squeeze the pit over the blender to get the juice out of that remaining flesh. Peel and add the garlic and ginger, finely grate in the zest of 2 limes and squeeze in their juice. Add the soy sauce and 1 teaspoon of peanut oil, then blitz until super-smooth. Pour into a large bowl.

To make a quick pickle, finely slice the mango skin and place in a shallow bowl. Halve the cucumber lengthways and scrape out the watery core, then finely slice with the chile and add to the bowl. Toss with the vinegar and a good pinch of sea salt to draw out excess moisture (you'll drain the liquor off, so don't worry about the amount of salt).

Preheat the broiler to high. Slice the skin off the salmon and reserve (or get your fishmonger to do this for you). Toss the fillets in the sauce, then lay them on the rice. Trim the scallions and chop at an angle into ¾-inch chunks, cut the broccoli into bite-sized florets, slicing the stalk, toss it all through the remaining sauce really well, then arrange around the salmon. Lay the salmon skins loosely on top, and place the pan under the broiler for 12 to 15 minutes, or until everything is just cooked through and nicely charred—keep an eye on it! Drain the pickle, pick and finely slice the mint leaves, toast the sesame seeds, toss together, and serve on the side. Finish each portion with a dollop of yogurt and serve with lime wedges, for squeezing over.

CALORIES	FAT	SAT FAT	PROTEIN	CARBS	SUGAR	SALT	FIBER	2 PORTIONS
597kcal	19.2g	3.9g	35.4g	74.7g	12.7g	1.4g	5.3g	VEG & FRUIT

GIANT MEATBALLS
SWEET TOMATO & JALAPEÑO SAUCE

These mighty balls prove that healthy doesn't have to mean small! Adding protein-packed black beans to the beef seriously ups the fiber level, helping our guts stay healthy and happy

SERVES 4

1 HOUR 20 MINUTES

1 lb lean ground beef

1 cup whole-grain bread crumbs

1 x 15-oz can of black beans

1 large egg

½ a bunch of fresh cilantro
   (½ oz)

3½ oz cottage cheese

1 tablespoon jarred sliced
   jalapeño chiles

2 x 14-oz cans of plum tomatoes

1 bunch of scallions

2 cloves of garlic

olive oil

1 cup brown rice

1 ripe mango

1 red pepper

2 limes

Preheat the oven to 350°F. Place the ground beef and bread crumbs in a food processor. Drain and add the black beans, crack in the egg, and add one-third of the cilantro and a pinch of sea salt and black pepper. Blitz until combined, then divide into four equal-sized patties. Divide up the cottage cheese, spooning it into the center of each patty, bring the mixture up and around it, then roll each one into a ball. Put aside.

To the empty food processor (there's no need to clean it), add the jalapeño chiles and 1 teaspoon of their pickling liquor, another third of the cilantro, and the canned tomatoes. Add the green top half of the scallions, peel and add the garlic, then blitz until smooth, taste, and season to perfection. Pour the sauce into a baking dish (12 x 8 inches) and sit the giant balls in it. Brush 1 teaspoon of oil over the balls and bake at the bottom of the oven for 35 minutes, or until cooked through and the sauce is bubbling.

Meanwhile, cook the rice in a pan of boiling salted water according to the package instructions. Peel the mango and place in a grill pan on a medium-high heat with the whole red pepper, the white halves of the scallions, and the halved limes, turning with tongs and removing to a board when charred all over. Pull the stalk and seeds out of the pepper and discard, cut all the charred mango flesh off the pit, then finely chop it all with the remaining third of the cilantro, mixing as you go. Carefully squeeze over the jammy juice of 1 lime, mix together, taste, and season to perfection. Serve the balls and tomato sauce on a bed of rice, with that zingy salsa on the side to pep things up, and the remaining lime in wedges for squeezing over.

CALORIES	FAT	SAT FAT	PROTEIN	CARBS	SUGAR	SALT	FIBER	3 PORTIONS
600kcal	13.7g	5g	44.5g	75.3g	15.7g	1.5g	13.4g	VEG & FRUIT

PERSIAN VEGGIE PILAF
SAFFRON, BLUEBERRIES, & BORLOTTI BEANS

As well as being super-tasty, jasmine rice is thought to stimulate the production of melatonin, the hormone linked to getting our bodies ready for sleep, making this a great dinner choice

SERVES 4

1 HOUR 10 MINUTES

1½ cups jasmine rice

2 cloves of garlic

½ a bunch of fresh Italian parsley (½ oz)

2 leeks

olive oil

1 lime

1 carrot

1 large bulb of fennel (14 oz)

1 veg or chicken bouillon cube

1 pinch of saffron

1 x 15-oz can of borlotti beans

5 oz blueberries

1 tablespoon blanched almonds

1 tablespoon shelled unsalted pistachios

4 tablespoons plain yogurt

Preheat the oven to 425°F. Wash the rice well in a sieve, then leave aside, slightly wet. Peel the garlic and finely slice with the parsley stalks. Wash and trim the leeks, then blitz in a food processor until finely chopped. Put a high-sided roasting pan (12 x 10 inches) on a medium-low heat with 4 tablespoons of oil. Stir in the garlic and parsley stalks, followed by the leeks, then finely grate over the lime zest, stirring occasionally. Peel the carrot, trim the fennel, then finely chop in the processor and stir those into the pan too, along with a good pinch of sea salt and black pepper. Fry for 15 minutes, or until soft but not colored, stirring regularly.

Crumble the bouillon cube into a pitcher, add the saffron and cover with 2¼ cups of boiling kettle water. Drain the beans and stir into the pan with the wet rice and blueberries. Pour over the stock, bring to a boil, then transfer to the oven for 30 minutes, or until crispy on top and the rice is cooked through.

Toast the almonds and pistachios until lightly golden, then crush in a pestle and mortar. Serve the pilaf sprinkled with the parsley leaves and crushed nuts, with a dollop of yogurt, and with lime wedges, for squeezing over.

CALORIES	FAT	SAT FAT	PROTEIN	CARBS	SUGAR	SALT	FIBER	3 PORTIONS
546kcal	18.4g	3g	15.5g	83.4g	10.9g	1.2g	10.5g	VEG & FRUIT

SICILIAN FISH BAKE
EGGPLANT, TOMATOES, PINE NUTS, & RAISINS

— White fish is a great, nutritious lean source of protein and is packed with lots of micronutrients, —
such as the mineral selenium, for cell protection and efficient immune system function

SERVES 4
1 HOUR 15 MINUTES

2 large eggplants

2 lbs ripe mixed-color tomatoes

1 red onion

4 cloves of garlic

1 celery heart

1 tablespoon dried oregano

1 pinch of dried red chili flakes

1 heaping teaspoon baby capers

1½ oz raisins

1½ oz pine nuts

4 black olives (with pits)

olive oil

4 x 4-oz white fish fillets,
   scaled, pin-boned

1 orange

1½ cups whole-wheat couscous

1½ oz arugula

4 tablespoons plain yogurt

Preheat the oven to 350°F. Very finely slice the eggplants and tomatoes into rounds. Peel and very finely slice the red onion and garlic. Trim the celery, halve, and finely slice lengthways. Throw it all into a large roasting pan with the oregano, chili flakes, capers, raisins, and pine nuts. Crush the olives with the heel of your hand, tear out the pits, then tear the flesh into the pan. Add 2 tablespoons of oil and a good pinch of sea salt and black pepper, then toss well. Arrange evenly, pulling a layer of tomatoes to the top, and bake on the bottom rack of the oven for 40 minutes.

Meanwhile, place the fish fillets in a sandwich bag, squeeze in the orange juice (reserving the halves), add a pinch of salt, and leave aside. When the time's up on the veg, remove from the oven and place the fish fillets on top, skin-side up. Drizzle over the orange juice, then return to the bottom rack of the oven for 15 more minutes, or until the fish is cooked through. Put the squeezed orange halves and couscous into a bowl, just cover the couscous with boiling kettle water, then pop a plate on top and leave to fluff up.

Sprinkle the arugula over the gorgeous traybake, fluff up the couscous, season to perfection, divide it all up, and serve each portion with a dollop of yogurt.

CALORIES	FAT	SAT FAT	PROTEIN	CARBS	SUGAR	SALT	FIBER	3 PORTIONS VEG & FRUIT
600kcal	18.5g	2.9g	37.1g	71.7g	25.1g	1.1g	9g	

GARLIC & THYME CHICKEN
MUSHROOMS, CHERRY TOMS, & ASPARAGUS

Trading up to whole-grain bread here means we can double our fiber intake, plus both whole-grain bread and chicken give us B vitamins, which are good for our metabolic systems

SERVES 4

30 MINUTES

2 tablespoons balsamic vinegar

olive oil

4 cloves of garlic

½ a bunch of fresh thyme (½ oz)

2 bunches of fine asparagus
   (12 oz)

12 oz ripe mixed-color cherry
   tomatoes, on the vine

4 x 4-oz boneless, skinless
   chicken breasts

4 large slices of whole-grain
   bread (2½ oz each)

4 medium mushrooms

3½ oz cream cheese

Preheat the oven to full whack (475°F). Mix the vinegar with 2 tablespoons of oil and a pinch of sea salt and black pepper in a large bowl. Crush the whole unpeeled garlic cloves with the heel of your knife and add to the bowl with the thyme sprigs. Trim the woody ends off the asparagus and pull the tomatoes off the vine, then toss in the marinade with the chicken.

Arrange the asparagus spears in a large roasting pan (16 x 12 inches) and add the slices of bread. Place a chicken breast on each slice, with a garlic clove and a few thyme sprigs on top. Trim the stalks and scruffy bits off the mushrooms, then place one on each chicken breast, stalk-side up, and divide the cream cheese between them. Scatter the tomatoes around the pan, drizzle over any remaining marinade, then roast hard and fast at the bottom of the oven for 20 to 25 minutes, or until the chicken is cooked through and everything is gnarly and delicious. Divide between your plates and tuck in.

CALORIES	FAT	SAT FAT	PROTEIN	CARBS	SUGAR	SALT	FIBER	2 PORTIONS VEG & FRUIT
480kcal	15.3g	4.1g	44.8g	38.8g	9.9g	1.5g	8.5g	

PORK MEATBALLS
SWEET ONION & APPLE GRAVY, BREAD BUNS

Meatballs get the super-food treatment here with a nutritious megamix of lean pork tenderloin, protein-rich cannellini beans, and fiber-packed oats, for a healthy heart and cholesterol level

SERVES 4

1 HOUR 15 MINUTES

1 bunch of fresh mint (1 oz)

1 x 15-oz can of cannellini beans

16-oz pork tenderloin

2 heaping teaspoons whole-grain mustard

½ cup rolled oats

olive oil

2 red onions

2 eating apples

1 tablespoon Worcestershire sauce

2 tablespoons all-purpose whole-grain flour

4 cups chicken stock

4 whole-grain buns

1 oz Cheddar cheese

3½ oz watercress and/or arugula

Preheat the oven to 400°F. Pick the mint leaves and put half into a food processor, popping the rest into a cup of cold water for later. Drain the beans, roughly chop the pork tenderloin, and add both to the processor with 1 heaping teaspoon of mustard, the oats, and a pinch of sea salt and black pepper. Blitz into a coarse grind (don't go too fine—keep it light and chunky in texture), then tip onto a board and roll into a long sausage. Chop into four equal pieces, divide each into five, and, with wet hands, roll into twenty balls.

To start your gravy, put 1 tablespoon of oil into a large high-sided roasting pan on a medium-high heat and add four of the balls, breaking them up with a wooden spoon. Peel and quarter the onions, break apart into petals, and add to the pan, stirring regularly. Cut the apples into thin wedges, discarding the core, and stir them in, too. Cook it all for 5 minutes, then stir in the Worcestershire sauce and the remaining heaping teaspoon of mustard, followed by the flour. Stir for 2 minutes, then gradually stir in the stock, season, and bring to a boil (it might seem like a lot of liquid, but it will reduce right down as it bakes). Plop in the remaining balls, spacing them out evenly, then transfer to the oven for 25 minutes, or until golden, shaking the pan halfway through. Warm the buns alongside for the last 5 minutes.

Remove the pan from the oven and finely grate the Cheddar over the balls to melt. Drain and toss the remaining mint leaves with the watercress and/or arugula, and serve it all together, dunking the buns in the gravy as you tuck in.

CALORIES	FAT	SAT FAT	PROTEIN	CARBS	SUGAR	SALT	FIBER	2 PORTIONS VEG & FRUIT
591kcal	15.7g	4.4g	49.1g	62.2g	15.6g	1.5g	13g	

JERK EGGPLANT & PEPPERS
RICE, BEANS, COCONUT, & CILANTRO

Giving attitude to this punchy jerk marinade, both garlic and ginger (even though they're small in size) are a source of potassium, which our muscles need to function properly

SERVES 4

1 HOUR 10 MINUTES

1 large eggplant

2 large mixed-color peppers

6 fresh bay leaves

½ a bunch of fresh thyme (½ oz)

6 cloves of garlic

2½-inch piece of fresh gingerroot

½–1 fresh Scotch bonnet chile

2 level teaspoons ground allspice

olive oil

2 tablespoons white wine vinegar

2 oz coconut cream

1½ cups white rice

1 x 15-oz can of kidney beans

4 tablespoons plain yogurt

½ a bunch of fresh cilantro (½ oz)

1 lime

Preheat the oven to 400°F. Trim the eggplant, quarter lengthways, and place in a large roasting pan (16 x 12 inches). Halve the peppers, seed, and add to the pan. Remove the stalks from the bay leaves, placing the leaves in a pestle and mortar with a good pinch of sea salt. Pound really well into a paste, then strip in the thyme leaves. Peel, roughly chop, and add the garlic and ginger, then seed and add the chile (wear gloves, if you want), along with the allspice. Bash well, then muddle in 1 tablespoon of oil and the vinegar. Spoon over the veg, mix well, and roast for 30 minutes.

In a bowl, whisk the coconut cream, rice, a pinch of salt, and 2½ cups of boiling water together. Remove the pan from the oven and carefully lift the veggies out of the pan for a moment. Drain and add the beans, then pour in the rice mixture and stir around with a wooden spoon to pick up any sticky bits from the bottom of the pan. Sit the veg back in the pan, pushing them down and curling the eggplant whichever way you like. Return to the bottom of the oven for another 25 minutes, or until the rice is cooked through.

Divide and spoon the yogurt into the peppers, then pick and push in the cilantro, portion up, and serve with lime wedges, for squeezing over.

CALORIES	FAT	SAT FAT	PROTEIN	CARBS	SUGAR	SALT	FIBER	2 PORTIONS VEG & FRUIT
481kcal	11.2g	5.9g	14.5g	80.5g	9.8g	0.6g	5.9g	

BRAZILIAN FISH BAKE
PEPPERS, CHILES, TOMATOES, & PAPRIKA

— Lots of fish, including red mullet and scallops, are a source of phosphorus—this mighty —
mineral makes up the walls of our cells, and ensures they are functioning efficiently

SERVES 6

50 MINUTES

1¾ lbs mixed fish fillets and
  seafood, such as red mullet,
  halibut, scallops, squid tubes

1 lemon

1 lime

sweet smoked paprika

3 mixed-color peppers

2 red onions

1¾ lbs ripe mixed-color tomatoes

1 fresh Scotch bonnet chile

1 x 14-oz can of light coconut
  milk

olive oil

1 bunch of fresh cilantro (1 oz)

2¼ cups brown rice

6 tablespoons plain yogurt

Preheat the oven to 350°F. Either ask your fishmonger to do you a nice mixture of fish and seafood and prep it all for you, cutting it into bite-sized chunks, or do it yourself at home. In a bowl, finely grate the lemon and lime zest over the fish, then squeeze over all the juice. Add ½ a teaspoon of paprika and a good pinch of sea salt and black pepper, then mix well.

Slice the peppers into ¼-inch-thick rounds, pulling out the seeds when you get to them. Peel the onions and finely slice into rounds with the tomatoes. Seed and finely slice the chile (wear gloves, if you want). Arrange a layer of tomatoes over the base of a roasting dish (12 x 10 inches). Cover with a double layer of peppers and a layer of onions, separating the slices into rings. Sprinkle over a pinch of paprika and black pepper, then add a random layer of fish, seafood, and a little chile. Keep repeating your layers, adding little pinches of paprika and black pepper as you go. Pour over any remaining citrus juices and add a pinch of sea salt. Use your fingers to push and poke everything down in the dish, then pour over the coconut milk and drizzle with 1 tablespoon of oil. Roughly chop the top leafy half of the cilantro and scatter most of it over the top. Cover with aluminum foil and bake for 20 minutes, then remove the foil and cook for another 15 minutes, or until cooked through.

Meanwhile, cook the rice in a large pan of boiling salted water according to the package instructions, then drain. Divide the rice between your bowls and spoon the traybake on top, making sure you ladle over that flavorsome broth, too. Top each portion with a dollop of yogurt, sprinkle with the remaining cilantro, and finish with an extra pinch of paprika, for an added kick.

CALORIES	FAT	SAT FAT	PROTEIN	CARBS	SUGAR	SALT	FIBER	2 PORTIONS
563kcal	15.2g	5.1g	33.9g	77g	15.5g	1.1g	6.6g	VEG & FRUIT

PASTA & RISOTTO

Amazing, tasty dishes celebrating two
of our favorite pantry staples

VEGGIE BOLOGNESE
LOADSA VEG, LENTILS, & PARMESAN

Embracing copper-rich lentils here instead of ground beef still gives us a nice hit of protein, ups our fiber intake, and also lowers the sat-fat levels we would usually find in a Bolognese

SERVES 6

1 HOUR 15 MINUTES

¾ oz dried porcini mushrooms

2 large red onions

2 cloves of garlic

2 carrots

2 stalks of celery

2 sprigs of fresh rosemary

olive oil

1 fresh bay leaf

½ cup Chianti

1 x 15-oz can of green lentils

2 x 14-oz cans of plum tomatoes

16 oz dried whole-wheat spaghetti

½ a bunch of fresh Italian parsley (½ oz)

3½ oz Parmesan cheese

In a small bowl, just cover the porcini with boiling kettle water to rehydrate them. Peel the onions, garlic, and carrots, trim the celery, and finely chop it all with the rosemary leaves. Place a large casserole pan on a medium-low heat with 1 tablespoon of oil, then add the chopped veg, rosemary, and the bay. Cook with a lid on for 20 minutes, or until softened, stirring occasionally.

Scoop out and finely chop the porcini and add to the pan with the soaking water, leaving any gritty bits behind. Turn the heat up to medium-high, pour in the Chianti, then leave to cook away. Tip in the lentils (juice and all), and the tomatoes, breaking them up with a wooden spoon. Half-fill each tomato can with water, swirl around, and pour into the pan. Bring to a boil, then reduce to a medium-low heat and simmer for 35 minutes, or until thick and delicious. Taste and season to perfection.

Meanwhile, cook the spaghetti in a large pan of boiling salted water according to the package instructions, then drain, reserving a cupful of cooking water. Toss the spaghetti through the Bolognese, loosening with a little reserved water, if needed. Finely chop the top leafy half of the parsley, finely grate over most of the Parmesan, and stir both through the pasta, then divide between your plates, grate over the rest of the Parmesan, and tuck in.

CALORIES	FAT	SAT FAT	PROTEIN	CARBS	SUGAR	SALT	FIBER	3 PORTIONS VEG & FRUIT
441kcal	9.8g	4g	22g	67.2g	12.7g	0.8g	11.4g	

JOOLS' TUNA PASTA BAKE
SWEET LEEKS, FENNEL, & TOMATOES

Canned tuna is a fantastic pantry staple and the hero in this super-popular dish. Tuna gives us selenium, which helps to protect our cells, and gives us strong, healthy skin and hair

SERVES 4

1 HOUR 10 MINUTES

4 black olives (with pits)

4 cloves of garlic

olive oil

2 leeks

1 bulb of fennel

2 x 14-oz cans of plum tomatoes

2 x 6-oz cans of tuna in
   spring water

10 oz dried whole-wheat pasta

½ a bunch of fresh Italian
   parsley (½ oz)

5 oz cottage cheese

¾ oz Parmesan cheese

Tear up the olives, discarding the pits, then peel and finely slice the garlic. Place a large pan on a medium heat with 1 tablespoon of oil, the olives, and garlic. Cook and stir while you trim, wash, and finely chop the leeks and fennel, adding them to the pan as you go. Cook with the lid on for 15 minutes, or until softened, stirring regularly.

Preheat the oven to 350°F. Tip the tomatoes into the pan, breaking them up with a wooden spoon, then just over half-fill one of the empty cans with water, swirl around, and pour into the pan. Drain and flake in the tuna, then simmer for 10 minutes while you parboil the pasta in a large pan of boiling salted water for 5 minutes, and drain (I like to make this dish a bit more fun by smashing up a mixture of pasta shapes, plus it's a great way of using up any odds and ends of pasta packages you've got in the cupboard).

Finely chop the top leafy half of the parsley and stir through the sauce with the cottage cheese and drained pasta, then taste and season to perfection. Tip into a baking dish, finely grate over the Parmesan, and bake for 30 minutes, or until golden and bubbling. Nice with a simple green salad on the side.

CALORIES	FAT	SAT FAT	PROTEIN	CARBS	SUGAR	SALT	FIBER	3 PORTIONS
500kcal	10.3g	3.3g	41.7g	63.8g	14.7g	1.3g	12g	VEG & FRUIT

SQUASH & SAUSAGE RISOTTO
RADICCHIO, THYME, & PARMESAN

A little sausage goes a long way in this delicious dish. I've paired it with sweet squash, which gives us a hit of vitamins A and C, both of which we need to keep our skin nice and healthy

SERVES 4

55 MINUTES

4 chipolata or small pork
  sausages

olive oil

1 teaspoon fennel seeds

½ teaspoon dried red chili flakes

½ a butternut squash (1¼ lbs)

2 onions

5 cups veg or chicken stock

½ cup Chianti

1½ cups Arborio risotto rice

1 radicchio or 2 red endive

10 oz cottage cheese

½ oz Parmesan cheese

2 sprigs of fresh thyme

Finely slice the chipolatas and place in a large high-sided pan on a medium heat with 1 tablespoon of oil, the fennel seeds, and chili flakes. Stir and fry while you chop the squash into ½-inch dice (leaving the skin on and seeding), and peel and finely chop the onions. Stir the veg into the pan, then cook with a lid ajar for around 20 minutes, or until the squash is starting to break down and caramelize, stirring regularly. Simmer the stock in a pan on a low heat.

Push the squash aside, and pour the Chianti into the pan. Let it cook away, picking up all that goodness from the base of the pan. Stir in the rice for 2 minutes, then gradually add the stock, a ladleful at a time, stirring and waiting for each ladleful to be absorbed before adding the next. Repeat this, stirring and massaging the starch out of the rice, for 20 minutes, or until the rice is cooked but still holding its shape, and the risotto is oozy.

Finely slice the radicchio or endive and stir through the risotto with the cottage cheese, then taste and season to perfection. Portion up and serve with a fine grating of Parmesan and a sprinkling of picked thyme leaves.

Veggie swap in

To make this recipe veggie, simply swap out the sausage for 1 x 15-oz can of borlotti beans and add them with the rice.

CALORIES	FAT	SAT FAT	PROTEIN	CARBS	SUGAR	SALT	FIBER	2 PORTIONS VEG & FRUIT
600kcal	15.6g	5.1g	31.1g	79.6g	12.2g	1.2g	3.9g	

SPAGHETTI ROSSO
GOLDEN CHICKEN & CHARRED GREEN VEG

Super-popular chicken breasts are high in vitamin B₆ and niacin, helping us think properly, and also contain the mineral phosphorus, which helps keep our bones strong and healthy

SERVES 4

30 MINUTES

1 bunch of scallions

1 bunch of asparagus (12 oz)

2 x 7-oz boneless, skinless
  chicken breasts

olive oil

5 cloves of garlic

1 lemon

1 bunch of fresh thyme (1 oz)

10 oz dried whole-wheat spaghetti

8 sun-dried tomatoes in oil

4 large roasted peeled red
  peppers in brine (12 oz)

½ teaspoon dried chili flakes

2 sprigs of fresh basil

Trim the scallions and the woody ends off the asparagus, then place in a large dry frying pan on a medium-high heat and let the veg start to char, tossing occasionally. Meanwhile, open out the chicken breasts, then bash and flatten the thicker end with the bottom of a pan, to roughly ¾ inch thick. Drizzle with 1 tablespoon of oil and a pinch of sea salt and black pepper. Crush and add 4 cloves of garlic, peel over the lemon zest in strips, and scatter over the thyme sprigs, then rub and toss in all that flavor.

When the veg are charred and nutty, remove to a plate and put the chicken, crushed garlic, lemon peel, and thyme into the pan. Cook the chicken for 8 minutes, or until golden and cooked through, turning every couple of minutes. When the chicken is looking good, return the veg to the pan to warm through, then switch off, keeping warm until needed.

Meanwhile, cook the spaghetti in a large pan of boiling salted water according to the package instructions. Peel the remaining clove of garlic and place in a food processor with the sun-dried tomatoes. Drain the peppers, quickly pat dry with paper towel, then add to the processor with the chili flakes and a pinch of black pepper. Blitz until smooth. Drain the pasta, reserving a cupful of cooking water, then return to the pan and toss with the sauce over a medium heat, loosening with a little reserved water, if needed. Slice the chicken ½ inch thick at an angle, toss in any nice pan juices, and serve with the pasta and veg, sprinkled with picked basil leaves, and with lemon wedges, for squeezing over.

CALORIES	FAT	SAT FAT	PROTEIN	CARBS	SUGAR	SALT	FIBER	2 PORTIONS
460kcal	14.5g	2.3g	26.9g	58.7g	8.6g	1.2g	7.4g	VEG & FRUIT

SCRUFFY WINTER LASAGNE
SAVOY CABBAGE & CREAMY CHICKEN STEW

— Most mushrooms are a source of B vitamins, which we need to keep our metabolic and nervous — systems healthy. They're also a source of potassium, which we need for healthy blood pressure

SERVES 8

2 HOURS 20 MINUTES

olive oil

8 skinless, boneless chicken
   thighs

2 leeks

2 stalks of celery

2 bulbs of fennel

4 rashers of smoked bacon

2 fresh bay leaves

½ a bunch of fresh thyme (½ oz)

2 heaping tablespoons
   all-purpose whole-grain flour

2 heaping teaspoons English
   mustard

1 liter reduced-fat (2%) milk

1 medium Savoy cabbage

14 oz baby chestnut or cremini
   mushrooms

1 lb fresh lasagne sheets

1 oz Parmesan cheese

1 loaf of whole-grain bread

Place a large casserole pan on a high heat with 1 tablespoon of oil. Brown the chicken thighs on all sides, stirring occasionally, while you wash, trim, and finely slice the leeks, celery, and fennel, and put aside. Finely slice the bacon and stir into the pan with the bay leaves, strip in the thyme leaves, and fry until the bacon is lightly golden. Stir in the sliced veg and fry for 15 minutes, stirring often, then stir in the flour, mustard, and a pinch of sea salt and black pepper. Gradually stir in the milk, reduce to a low heat, cover, and simmer for 20 minutes, stirring regularly.

Click off and wash the green outer leaves of the cabbage (12 oz in total), saving the rest for another day. Line up the leaves, cut out and discard the stalks, then slice ¾ inch thick. Finely slice the mushrooms and stir into the stew with the cabbage and 2⅓ cups of boiling water. Simmer for 30 more minutes. Preheat the oven to 350°F.

Turn the heat off under the stew and use two forks to shred the chicken, if needed, then taste and season to perfection. Ladle a layer of stew into a roasting pan (14 x 10 inches). Roughly tear in a couple of sheets of pasta, then repeat the process until you've used it all up. Press and push your fingers into it to create texture—you want it scruffy—then finely grate over the Parmesan. Bake for 40 minutes, or until golden and bubbling. Leave to sit for 5 minutes, then serve with the bread on the side, for dunking.

CALORIES	FAT	SAT FAT	PROTEIN	CARBS	SUGAR	SALT	FIBER	3 PORTIONS
501kcal	15.8g	5.8g	35g	54.2g	13g	1.5g	9.6g	VEG & FRUIT

TOMATO RISOTTO
GARLICKY BASIL SAUCE

___ Our humble friend the tomato packs a real punch of vitamin C, one function of which is to protect ___
our cells by working as an antioxidant, to reverse or prevent damage from external factors

SERVES 4

30 MINUTES

2 onions

2 carrots

2 stalks of celery

olive oil

5 cups veg stock

1 x 14-oz can of plum tomatoes

1 bunch of fresh basil (1 oz)

1 clove of garlic

extra virgin olive oil

1⅓ cups Arborio risotto rice

½ a fresh red chile

10 oz cottage cheese

Peel the onions and carrots, trim the celery, then finely chop it all and place in a large high-sided pan on a medium heat with 1 tablespoon of olive oil. Cook for 10 minutes, or until softened, stirring occasionally. Simmer the stock and canned tomatoes together in a pan on a low heat.

Pick the baby basil leaves into a cup of cold water, then rip the top leafy half of the bunch into a blender, chucking the stalks into your stock. Peel the garlic and add to the blender, cover with half a ladleful of hot stock, and blitz until smooth. Add 2 tablespoons of extra virgin olive oil, blitz again, taste, and season to perfection to make your sauce.

Stir the rice into the veg for 2 minutes, then gradually add the tomatoey stock through a sieve, a ladleful at a time, really pushing the tomatoes through the sieve, stirring and waiting for each ladleful to be absorbed before adding the next. Repeat this, stirring and massaging the starch out of the rice, for 20 minutes, or until the rice is cooked but still holding its shape, and the risotto is oozy. Seed and finely chop the chile, then stir through the risotto with the cottage cheese. Taste and season to perfection. Divide up, top with the garlicky basil sauce, and scatter over the reserved basil leaves.

CALORIES	FAT	SAT FAT	PROTEIN	CARBS	SUGAR	SALT	FIBER	3 PORTIONS VEG & FRUIT
516kcal	15.4g	4.2g	17.1g	77.7g	14.8g	0.6g	4.1g	

GARLIC MUSHROOM PASTA
CREAMY THYME & TRUFFLE SAUCE

— Most common mushrooms—the types we find in the shops—are packed with the mineral copper, which we need to keep all the connective tissue in our bodies strong and healthy —

SERVES 4

30 MINUTES

4 cloves of garlic

2 red onions

olive oil

½ a bunch of fresh thyme (½ oz)

½ teaspoon dried red chili flakes

12 oz baby chestnut or cremini mushrooms

10 oz dried whole-wheat fusilli

1 heaping tablespoon all-purpose whole-grain flour

1⅔ cups reduced-fat (2%) milk

1 teaspoon truffle oil

10 oz cottage cheese

½ a bunch of fresh Italian parsley (½ oz)

1 lemon

¾ oz Parmesan cheese

Peel and finely slice the garlic and onions, then place in a large casserole pan on a medium heat with 1 tablespoon of oil. Strip in the thyme leaves, then add the chili flakes and cook for 10 minutes, or until very lightly golden, stirring occasionally. Meanwhile, slice the mushrooms as finely as you can, chuck three-quarters into the pan and put the rest aside (this will give you a lovely contrast between the earthy depth of flavor from the cooked mushrooms in the sauce and the raw, nutty, clean-tasting mushrooms that you'll add later).

Cook the pasta in a large pan of boiling salted water according to the package instructions, then drain well, reserving a cupful of cooking water.

Stir the flour into the veg pan for 1 minute, then pour in the milk and simmer for 5 minutes. Carefully pour the mixture into a blender with the truffle oil and blitz until smooth (the trick with truffle oil is to use it subtly like this to prop up the other flavors, not overtake them). Return the sauce to the pan and add the drained pasta and the cottage cheese. Finely chop and add the top leafy half of the parsley, then stir it all together, loosening with a little reserved water, if needed. Taste and season to perfection, stir through the reserved sliced raw mushrooms, divide between your plates, and finish with a fine grating of lemon zest and Parmesan.

CALORIES	FAT	SAT FAT	PROTEIN	CARBS	SUGAR	SALT	FIBER	2 PORTIONS VEG & FRUIT
498kcal	14.4g	5.8g	25.9g	69.8g	14.7g	0.8g	10g	

PASTA AGRODOLCE
SWEET PEPPERS, SALTED RICOTTA, & BASIL

Colorful sweet peppers are super-high in vitamin C—with much higher levels than a lot of other fruit and veg—meaning this dish is perfect for giving our immune systems a nice boost

SERVES 4

50 MINUTES

2 red onions

2 red peppers

2 yellow peppers

1¾ oz pine nuts

olive oil

4 cloves of garlic

1 teaspoon fennel seeds

½ teaspoon dried red chili flakes

½ a cinnamon stick

4 oz raisins

4 tablespoons balsamic vinegar

2 x 14-oz cans of plum tomatoes

10 oz dried whole-wheat penne

2½ oz salted ricotta or feta
   cheese

4 sprigs of fresh basil

Peel the onions, then place in a large pan of boiling salted water with the whole peppers. Sit something on top, like a colander, so the veg stay submerged, and boil for 15 minutes. Use tongs to gently and carefully remove the onions and peppers to a pan, leaving the water on the lowest heat. Pull the stalks and seeds out of the peppers and discard, and as soon as they're cool enough to handle, roughly chop the onions and peppers.

Lightly toast the pine nuts in a large casserole pan on a medium heat until golden, tossing often, then remove to a plate. Add 1 tablespoon of oil to the casserole pan, then finely slice and add the garlic, along with the fennel seeds, chili flakes, and cinnamon stick. Once the mixture is lightly golden, finely chop the raisins and stir into the pan with the onions and peppers to cook for 10 minutes, stirring regularly. When it's all starting to catch and caramelize, add the balsamic and the canned tomatoes, breaking up the tomatoes with a wooden spoon. Just under half-fill each can with water, swirl around, and pour into the pan. Bring to a boil, then simmer for 15 minutes, stirring occasionally. Taste and season to perfection, then discard the cinnamon stick.

Meanwhile, bring the pan of water back up to a boil, cook the pasta according to the package instructions, then drain, reserving a cupful of cooking water. Toss the pasta through the sauce, loosening with a little reserved water, if needed. Crumble or grate over the cheese and serve scattered with pine nuts and picked basil leaves.

CALORIES	FAT	SAT FAT	PROTEIN	CARBS	SUGAR	SALT	FIBER	4 PORTIONS
600kcal	16.7g	2.7g	19.3g	99.4g	49.6g	0.4g	14g	VEG & FRUIT

SUPER GREENS CANNELLONI
CREAMY RICOTTA & BASIL SAUCE

This beautiful dish celebrates leafy seasonal greens—they're packed full of nutrients such as folic acid, which our bodies need to make red blood cells, keeping us awake and alert

SERVES 6

1 HOUR 30 MINUTES

2 onions

6 cloves of garlic

olive oil

16 oz fresh seasonal greens, such
   as kale, chard, cavolo nero,
   nettles, arugula, borage

16 oz frozen chopped spinach

1 whole nutmeg, for grating

½ a lemon

8 oz dried cannelloni tubes

1 fresh red chile

1 bunch of fresh basil (1 oz)

3 x 14-oz cans of plum tomatoes

1 oz Parmesan cheese

8 oz ricotta cheese

1 large egg

¾ cup reduced-fat (2%) milk

Peel and finely slice the onions and 4 cloves of garlic and place in a large non-stick pan on a medium heat with 1 tablespoon of oil. Cook and stir while you prep the fresh greens—wash the leaves, trimming away any tough stalks. Slice the leaves and stir into the pan with the frozen spinach and a good grating of nutmeg. Cook for 15 minutes, or until nice and dark, stirring regularly. Tip into a food processor, finely grate in the lemon zest, add a squeeze of juice, then blitz until finely chopped. Taste and season to perfection, then, once cool enough to handle, pop the greens into a big sandwich bag, snip off the corner, and pipe into the cannelloni tubes.

Preheat the oven to 350°F. Return the pan to the heat (there's no need to clean it) with 1 tablespoon of oil. Peel the remaining garlic, finely slice with the chile and basil stalks, add to the pan, and fry until lightly golden. Pour in the tomatoes, breaking them up with a wooden spoon. Half-fill the cans with water, swirl around, and pour into the pan. Bring to a boil, then simmer for 10 minutes. Taste and season to perfection—you want the sauce quite wet, as the pasta will soak lots of it up. Pour into a baking dish (12 x 10 inches) and line up the filled cannelloni on top, pushing them into the sauce.

Finely grate the Parmesan into the food processor (there's no need to clean it). Add the ricotta, egg, milk, the basil leaves, and a pinch of sea salt and black pepper, and blitz until smooth. Pour it over the cannelloni, making sure all the tubes are covered, then bake on the bottom rack of the oven for 40 minutes, or until cooked through. Serve with hunks of brown bread with seeds to up your carb intake, and a fresh side salad of your choice.

CALORIES	FAT	SAT FAT	PROTEIN	CARBS	SUGAR	SALT	FIBER	3 PORTIONS
383kcal	12.8g	5.4g	21.2g	46.4g	14.8g	0.7g	7.6g	VEG & FRUIT

SAUSAGE PASTA
BROCCOLI, CHILE, & SWEET TOMATOES

Super-nutritious broccoli is packed with vitamin K, keeping our bones strong and healthy, and contains folic acid and vitamin C, boosting our immune systems and helping us think properly

SERVES 4

45 MINUTES

12 oz broccoli

4 chipolata or small pork
 sausages

1–2 fresh red chiles

olive oil

2 teaspoons fennel seeds

4 cloves of garlic

2 onions

½ a bunch of fresh oregano (½ oz)

2 tablespoons red wine vinegar

1 x 14-oz can of plum tomatoes

10 oz dried whole-wheat
 tagliatelle

1½ oz Parmesan cheese

Chop the broccoli florets off the stalk. Cut the woody end off the stalk, halve the stalk lengthways, and put into a large pan of boiling salted water with the sausages and whole chile(s). Pop the lid on, boil for 5 minutes, then remove, leaving the water on the lowest heat.

Meanwhile, chop the broccoli florets into nice bite-sized chunks and put aside for later. Once cool enough to handle, finely slice the sausages, broccoli stalk, and chile and place in a large frying pan on a medium heat with 1 tablespoon of oil, the fennel seeds, and a pinch of sea salt and black pepper. Stir and fry while you peel and finely slice the garlic and onions. Once the sausage is lightly golden, stir in the garlic, followed a minute later by the onions, then pick in the oregano leaves. Cook for 15 minutes, or until softened, stirring occasionally. Add the vinegar and cook completely away, then pour in the tomatoes, breaking them up with a wooden spoon. Half-fill the can with water, swirl around, and pour into the pan. Simmer for 15 more minutes, or until thickened, then taste and season to perfection.

Meanwhile, bring the pan of water back up to a boil, and cook the pasta according to the package instructions, adding the broccoli florets for the last 4 minutes. Drain the pasta and broccoli, reserving a cupful of cooking water. Toss through the sauce, loosening with a little reserved water, if needed. Finely grate in most of the Parmesan and toss together, then serve with the rest of the Parmesan grated over the top.

CALORIES	FAT	SAT FAT	PROTEIN	CARBS	SUGAR	SALT	FIBER	3 PORTIONS
502kcal	17g	5.7g	27g	64.3g	12.1g	1g	12.1g	VEG & FRUIT

SPINACH PICI PASTA
BABY ZUCCHINI, TOMATOES, & PINE NUTS

___ Protein-rich pine nuts are super-high in the mineral manganese, which we need to protect our ___
cells, and in heart-healthy unsaturated fats, which keep our blood cholesterol healthy

SERVES 4

50 MINUTES

7 oz baby spinach

2¼ cups Tipo OO or all-purpose
   flour, plus extra for dusting

olive oil

4 cloves of garlic

½ teaspoon dried red chili flakes

7 oz baby zucchini

11 oz ripe cherry tomatoes, on
   the vine

1¾ oz pine nuts

½ a bunch of fresh basil (½ oz)

1¾ oz Parmesan cheese

extra virgin olive oil

In a food processor, blitz the spinach and flour until a ball of dough forms, letting the machine do all the work. Touch the dough—it shouldn't be sticky, you want a playdough consistency, so add a little more flour if needed. To make the pici, simply tear off ¾-inch balls of dough and roll them out into long, thin sausage shapes—think fine green beans—on a clean surface (the beauty is that they're all different, so get little helpers involved, if you can). Cook the pici straight away, or leave them to dry out for a few hours, or even overnight.

Put a large pan of salted water on to boil. Put a large frying pan on a medium heat with 2 tablespoons of olive oil. Peel, finely slice, and add the garlic, along with the chili flakes. Finely slice and add the zucchini, then halve and add the tomatoes. Cook it all for 5 minutes, then stir in the pine nuts and add a ladleful of boiling water. Leave on the lowest heat while you cook the pasta.

Add the pici to your pan of boiling salted water. If it's freshly rolled it will only need about 5 minutes, but if you've let it dry give it 8 to 10 minutes, checking on it to make sure you get lovely al dente pasta. Drain, reserving a cupful of cooking water, then toss through the veg. Reserving the baby basil leaves, finely slice the bigger ones and stir into the pan with most of the finely grated Parmesan, loosening with a little reserved water, if needed. Divide between your warm plates and serve with a few drips of extra virgin olive oil, with the remaining Parmesan and the baby basil leaves sprinkled over.

CALORIES	FAT	SAT FAT	PROTEIN	CARBS	SUGAR	SALT	FIBER	2 PORTIONS
500kcal	21.6g	4.3g	20.2g	56.6g	5.8g	0.4g	4.7g	VEG & FRUIT

SPAGHETTI CAKE
SWEET EGGPLANT & TOMATO

— The bonus of choosing whole-grain spaghetti over white is that it can contain more than double —
the amount of fiber, as well as lots of B vitamins, which keep our metabolic systems healthy

SERVES 4

1 HOUR 30 MINUTES

1 large eggplant (12 oz)

10 oz dried whole-wheat spaghetti

olive oil

4 sprigs of fresh oregano

2 red onions

½–1 fresh red chile

1 x 14-oz can of plum tomatoes

10 oz cottage cheese

2 large eggs

1 oz Parmesan cheese

1 lemon

2½ oz arugula

1 tablespoon balsamic vinegar

------- *Get ahead* -------
Make this earlier in the
day and simply keep in
the fridge until you're
ready to bake.

Preheat the oven to 350°F. Place the whole eggplant in a large pan of boiling salted water. Sit something on top, like a colander, so the eggplant stays submerged, cook for 15 minutes, then remove to a board. Add the spaghetti to the water and cook according to the package instructions, then drain and place in a large bowl to cool.

Meanwhile, roughly chop the eggplant about ½ inch thick. Place a deep 10½-inch non-stick ovenproof frying pan on a medium heat with 1 tablespoon of oil and the eggplant, then pick in the oregano leaves. Peel the onions, then finely slice with the chile and add to the pan. Cook for 15 minutes, or until golden and gnarly, stirring regularly. Pour in the canned tomatoes, breaking them up with a wooden spoon, then just under half-fill the can with water, swirl around, and pour into the pan. Bring to a boil, then simmer gently for 10 minutes, or until thick. Taste and season to perfection.

Pour the tomato sauce over the spaghetti, add the cottage cheese, crack in the eggs, finely grate in most of the Parmesan, then mix together really well. Pour the spaghetti mixture back into the pan, pushing it into an even layer and packing it up at the sides. Get it going over a medium heat on the stove for 2 minutes, then bake at the bottom of the oven for 40 minutes, or until golden all over. Bang out onto a board, grate over the remaining Parmesan, and serve with lemon-dressed arugula and a drizzle of balsamic.

CALORIES	FAT	SAT FAT	PROTEIN	CARBS	SUGAR	SALT	FIBER	3 PORTIONS
496kcal	15.7g	5.8g	26.7g	66.2g	15g	0.9g	8.7g	VEG & FRUIT

PEA & SPINACH RISOTTO
MINT, COTTAGE CHEESE, & PARMESAN

The freezer is your best friend in this celebration of sweet peas and mighty spinach, both of which give us a hit of vitamins C and K, keeping our bones strong and healthy

SERVES 4
40 MINUTES

1 onion

2 stalks of celery

olive oil

5 cups veg stock

1½ cups Arborio risotto rice

12 oz frozen chopped spinach

3½ cups frozen baby peas

10 oz cottage cheese

½ a bunch of fresh mint (½ oz)

½ oz Parmesan cheese

Peel the onion, trim the celery, then finely chop both and place in a large high-sided pan on a medium heat with 1 tablespoon of oil. Cook for 10 minutes, or until softened, stirring occasionally. Simmer the stock in a pan on a low heat.

Stir the rice and spinach into the veg for 2 minutes, then gradually add the stock, a ladleful at a time, stirring and waiting for each ladleful to be absorbed before adding the next. Repeat this, stirring and massaging the starch out of the rice, for 20 minutes, or until the rice is cooked but still holding its shape, and the risotto is oozy, adding half the peas for the last few minutes.

Blitz the cottage cheese with the rest of the peas and most of the picked mint leaves in a food processor until smooth. Stir most of the creamy curds through the risotto, taste, and season to perfection, then divide between your plates. Serve with a dollop of creamy curds, a fine grating of Parmesan, and with the remaining mint leaves scattered over.

CALORIES	FAT	SAT FAT	PROTEIN	CARBS	SUGAR	SALT	FIBER	3 PORTIONS VEG & FRUIT
517kcal	12.1g	4.6g	24.8g	76.8g	7.4g	0.5g	8.3g	

SQUASH MAC 'N' CHEESE
CRISPY CRUMBS & POPPED BEANS

Embracing veg and using squash to create a creamy, comforting sauce means we can cut right back on the cheese and lose the butter usually used in mac 'n' cheese

SERVES 6

1 HOUR 30 MINUTES

1 leek

1 onion

olive oil

1 butternut squash (2½ lbs)

1 heaping tablespoon all-purpose whole-grain flour

2 cups reduced-fat (2%) milk

16 oz dried macaroni

2 heaping teaspoons English mustard

10 oz cottage cheese

1½ oz Parmesan cheese

1 x 15-oz can of cannellini beans

2 cloves of garlic

1 teaspoon dried red chili flakes

2 sprigs of fresh rosemary

1 slice of whole-grain bread (1¾ oz)

Wash and trim the leek, peel the onion, then finely chop and place in a pan on a medium heat with 1 tablespoon of oil. Cook and stir while you carefully halve the squash lengthways and seed, reserving the seedy core. Chop the squash into ¾-inch chunks, leaving the skin on, and stir into the pan. Cook for 10 minutes, then stir in the flour, followed by the milk and 2 cups of water. Simmer with a lid ajar for 35 minutes, or until the squash is cooked through, stirring occasionally.

Meanwhile, preheat the oven to 350°F. Parboil the macaroni in a large pan of boiling salted water for 5 minutes, then drain and tip back into the pan. Carefully pour the contents of the veg pan into a food processor and blitz until smooth (working in batches, if necessary) to make your sauce. Taste and season to perfection, then pour over the pasta, add the mustard and cottage cheese, finely grate over most of the Parmesan, and mix well. Transfer to a high-sided baking dish (16 x 12 inches), then grate over the remaining Parmesan. Bake for around 40 minutes, or until golden and bubbling.

With 15 minutes to go, drain the beans, then toast and dry fry them in a large frying pan on a medium-high heat for 5 minutes, or until popped, shaking occasionally. Peel the garlic and put in the processor with the chili flakes, seedy squash core, rosemary leaves, and bread and blitz into crumbs. Add to the beans, then toast and toss until crisp and gnarly. Serve the pasta with the toasted beans and crumbs on the side. Good with a lemon-dressed salad.

CALORIES	FAT	SAT FAT	PROTEIN	CARBS	SUGAR	SALT	FIBER	2 PORTIONS VEG & FRUIT
566kcal	11.2g	4.6g	26.2g	94.4g	19.8g	0.8g	10g	

SHRIMP & FENNEL RISOTTO
CRISPY PANCETTA & CHILE SPRINKLES

Popular shrimp are super-high in vitamin B$_{12}$, which our bodies need to make red blood cells, while fragrant fennel gives us potassium, helping to keep our blood pressure in check

SERVES 4

40 MINUTES

2 onions

1 bulb of fennel

2 rashers of smoked pancetta

olive oil

7½ oz large raw peeled shrimp

4 cups veg stock

1 clove of garlic

1 fresh red chile

14 oz ripe cherry tomatoes, on the vine

1½ cups Arborio risotto rice

½ a bunch of fresh Italian parsley (½ oz)

1 lemon

10 oz cottage cheese

Peel and finely chop the onions, then trim and finely slice the fennel. Place the pancetta in a large high-sided pan on a medium heat until crispy and the fat has rendered out, then remove to a plate, leaving the flavorsome fat behind. Add the onions and fennel to the pan with 1 tablespoon of oil and a splash of water. Cook for 10 minutes, or until softened, stirring regularly.

Meanwhile, use a small sharp knife to lightly score down the back of the shrimp (and remove the vein, if needed), then put aside. Simmer the stock in a pan on a low heat with the peeled garlic clove and the halved, seeded chile. Prick each tomato with the tip of a knife and drop into the stock, adding the vines too for extra flavor. After 1 minute scoop out the tomatoes, then carefully pinch off and discard their skins.

Stir the rice into the veg for 2 minutes, then gradually add the stock through a sieve, a ladleful at a time, stirring and waiting for each ladleful to be absorbed before adding the next. Repeat this, stirring and massaging the starch out of the rice, for 20 minutes, or until the rice is cooked but still holding its shape, and the risotto is oozy. Stir in the shrimp and tomatoes for the last 5 minutes.

Meanwhile, pick the parsley leaves onto a board and finely grate over the lemon zest. Pick the chile halves and garlic out of the stock pan or sieve and add to the board with the crispy pancetta, then finely chop it all to make an amazing sprinkle. Stir the cottage cheese through the risotto, taste, and season to perfection, then serve scattered with the sprinkles.

CALORIES	FAT	SAT FAT	PROTEIN	CARBS	SUGAR	SALT	FIBER	2 PORTIONS VEG & FRUIT
501kcal	10.5g	3.7g	26.9g	75.2g	12.7g	0.8g	4.8g	

SQUASH & RICOTTA RAVIOLI
7-VEG TOMATO SAUCE, ARUGULA, & PARMESAN

Super-creamy ricotta is a great source of the minerals calcium and phosphorus, both of which are essential for healthy bones and teeth, plus it's lower in fat than most other cheeses

SERVES 4

2 HOURS 30 MINUTES

1 small butternut squash (2 lbs)

8 oz ricotta cheese

½ a bunch of fresh basil (½ oz)

3 large eggs

2¼ cups Tipo 00 or all-purpose flour, plus extra for dusting

2½ cups 7-veg tomato sauce (see page 234)

2½ oz arugula

⅓ oz Parmesan cheese

extra virgin olive oil

Preheat the oven to 350°F. In a pan, roast the squash whole for 1 hour. Add the ricotta and roast for another 30 minutes, or until the squash is cooked through. Halve it in the pan, discarding the skin and seeds. Pick, finely chop, and add the basil leaves, then mash it all with the ricotta, scraping up any sticky bits from the pan. Taste, season to perfection, and cool.

To make the pasta dough, put the eggs and flour into a food processor and whiz into a ball of dough. Knead on a flour-dusted surface until smooth. Cut in half, wrap in plastic wrap, and rest for 30 minutes.

Flatten one piece of dough by hand. Run it through the thickest setting on a pasta machine, then take the rollers down two settings and run it through again to make it thinner. Now fold it in half and run it back through the thickest setting again, repeating this a few times for super-smooth dough. Start rolling the sheet down through each setting, lightly dusting with flour as you go. Turn the crank with one hand while the other maintains just a little tension to avoid any kinks or folds. Take it right down to 1/32 inch, then lay the sheet flat and stamp out circles with a 5-inch cutter. Working quickly, spoon 1 heaping teaspoon of filling into the middle of each, lightly brush the exposed pasta with water, fold into half-moon shapes over the filling, gently pressing to squeeze out any air, and seal. Repeat with the second ball of dough.

Warm the sauce in a pan over a medium heat, and in batches cook the pasta in a large pan of boiling salted water for just 2 minutes. Toss the pasta with the sauce and arugula and serve with finely grated Parmesan, finished with a few drips of extra virgin olive oil.

CALORIES	FAT	SAT FAT	PROTEIN	CARBS	SUGAR	SALT	FIBER	3 PORTIONS VEG & FRUIT
536kcal	13.6g	5.8g	26g	79.7g	19.4g	0.5g	8.2g	

SOUPS

Hearty balanced bowlfuls that will
fill you up and tickle your taste buds

ALPHABET TOMATO SOUP
FRESH BASIL & CHEDDAR CHEESE

Lots of lovely fresh tomatoes, plus chile, gives us a big hit of vitamin C here—this keeps our blood vessels strong, so our hearts don't have to work as hard to pump blood around the body

SERVES 4

1 HOUR

2 red onions

2 carrots

2 stalks of celery

olive oil

½–1 fresh red chile

½ a bulb of garlic

½ a bunch of fresh basil (½ oz)

3 lbs ripe cherry tomatoes, on the vine

10 oz dried alphabet pasta

3 oz Cheddar cheese

The idea of this recipe is to get it all cooking fast, then let the heat do the work, giving a soup with a taste that will immediately remind you of that incredible smell of tomatoes growing in a greenhouse. Peel the onions, trim the carrots and celery, then chop into ¾-inch chunks and chuck into a large casserole pan on a medium-high heat with 1 tablespoon of oil. Seed and add the chile, then squash and add the whole unpeeled garlic cloves. Pick the baby basil leaves into a cup of cold water, then add the rest of the bunch (stalks and all—for massive extra flavor) to the pan. Wash and add the whole tomatoes (stalks, vines, and all). Stir for 5 minutes, then cover with 8 cups of water. Boil fast for 40 minutes, then turn the heat off.

Set up another pan alongside the soup with a coarse sieve in it. Ladle the chunky soup into the sieve, really crushing and pushing all that goodness through, leaving just the stalks, vines, and skins behind, which you can discard as you go. Bring up to a boil, stir in the pasta, and simmer until it's just cooked, then taste the soup and season to perfection. Serve sprinkled with grated cheese and the baby basil leaves.

Lovely leftovers

If you're not serving up all four portions at once, you'll find that left overnight in the fridge, the pasta sucks up even more of the soup, making it the perfect topping for a nice piece of whole-grain toast.

CALORIES	FAT	SAT FAT	PROTEIN	CARBS	SUGAR	SALT	FIBER	3 PORTIONS
487kcal	13.2g	5.4g	18.7g	78.3g	22.5g	0.6g	18.7g	VEG & FRUIT

SPINACH, MUSHROOM, & RISOTTO SOUP
SHATTERED PARMESAN & HAZELNUT CRISPS

With a whole 2 pounds of mighty spinach, this dish gives us a massive boost of micronutrients, particularly vitamin K, which our bodies need for good bone health and blood clotting

SERVES 4

50 MINUTES

2 onions

2 cloves of garlic

2 stalks of celery

2 tablespoons dried porcini
  mushrooms

2 sprigs of fresh rosemary

olive oil

4 large portobello mushrooms

1½ cups Arborio risotto rice

6 cups chicken or veg stock

2 lbs frozen chopped spinach

2 tablespoons blanched
  hazelnuts

2 oz Parmesan cheese

1 whole nutmeg, for grating

4 tablespoons plain yogurt

1 lemon

extra virgin olive oil

Preheat the oven to 350°F. Peel the onions and garlic, trim the celery, then finely chop with the porcini and rosemary leaves (or blitz in a food processor). Put a large pan on a medium-high heat with 1 tablespoon of olive oil. Tip in the prepped veg and cook for 10 minutes, or until softened, stirring occasionally. Finely chop the portobello mushrooms, then add to the pan for a further 10 minutes. Stir in the rice for 2 minutes, then pour in the stock, add the frozen spinach, and simmer for 20 minutes, stirring occasionally.

Meanwhile, bash up the hazelnuts until nice and fine in a pestle and mortar. Line a baking sheet (12 x 10 inches) with a sheet of parchment paper, then rub the paper with 1 teaspoon of olive oil. Finely grate the Parmesan over the surface in a thick, even layer, scatter over the hazelnuts, and finely grate over a little nutmeg. Pop into the oven for 12 minutes, or until dark golden—keep an eye on it! Once cool and set, crack into shards and peel off the paper.

Now, I like to blitz about a third of the soup in the pan with an immersion blender and stir it back through to give the whole thing a creamier texture, but you can leave it as it is, if you prefer. Taste and season to perfection, then divide between your bowls. Divide up the yogurt, add a squeeze of lemon juice, and drizzle each portion with 1 teaspoon of extra virgin olive oil (use new season's oil, if you can get it). Serve with the Parmesan and hazelnut crisps.

CALORIES	FAT	SAT FAT	PROTEIN	CARBS	SUGAR	SALT	FIBER	3 PORTIONS VEG & FRUIT
575kcal	19.4g	5.3g	26.6g	71.9g	9.4g	0.5g	10.2g	

PERUVIAN SWEET POTATO SOUP
CORN, PEPPERS, CHICKEN, & QUINOA

As well as giving us a nice hit of vitamin C, sweet potatoes also provide us with manganese, which we need to keep all the bones and connective tissue in our bodies strong and healthy

SERVES 4
1 HOUR 10 MINUTES

1 large red onion

2 cloves of garlic

2 mixed-color peppers

1 lb potatoes

1 lb sweet potatoes

1 fresh red chile

2 skinless, boneless chicken
  thighs

olive oil

1 pinch of cumin seeds

1 teaspoon coriander seeds

2 whole cloves

6 cups veg or chicken stock

2 corn on the cob

2 limes

¾ cup quinoa

1 bunch of fresh cilantro (1 oz)

3 oz feta cheese

Peel the onion, chop into ½-inch dice, then peel and finely chop the garlic. Seed the peppers, wash the spuds and sweet potatoes (leaving the skins on for extra nutritional benefit), and chop it all into ¾-inch dice. Chop the chile.

Put a large casserole pan on a medium-high heat. Finely slice the chicken thighs and place in the pan with 1 tablespoon of oil. Cook and stir while you pound the cumin and coriander seeds in a pestle and mortar with the cloves and a pinch of sea salt and black pepper, until fine. Tip the spice mixture into the pan, stirring regularly until the chicken is golden. Stir in all the prepped veg and cook for 15 minutes, stirring regularly. Pour in the stock, bring to a boil, then simmer for 30 minutes.

Use the heel of a large knife to chop the corn into ¾-inch rounds, carefully tapping it with a rolling pin to cut through the cob. Halve 1 lime and stir into the pan with the corn and quinoa. Cook for a final 15 minutes, or until the quinoa and corn are cooked through. Taste the soup and season to perfection. Finely chop the top leafy half of the cilantro, crumble the feta, then stir both through the soup, letting everything break up a bit so you get a nice range of textures. Serve with lime wedges, for squeezing over.

CALORIES	FAT	SAT FAT	PROTEIN	CARBS	SUGAR	SALT	FIBER	3 PORTIONS VEG & FRUIT
533kcal	14.3g	4.3g	24.5g	82.1g	18.2g	1.3g	10.2g	

BLACK BEAN SOUP
POACHED EGGS, SALSA, & TORTILLAS

— This classic Costa Rican soup heroes humble black beans—they're really high in protein, as well as dietary fiber, which keeps our gut healthy and keeps us regular! We like that —

SERVES 4

50 MINUTES

2 red onions

2 cloves of garlic

2 stalks of celery

2 mixed-color peppers

olive oil

2 fresh bay leaves

2 fresh red chiles

2 sprigs of fresh thyme

2 x 15-oz cans of black beans

4 large eggs

½ a bunch of fresh cilantro (½ oz)

1½ oz feta cheese

½ a lime

4 corn tortillas

Peel the onions and garlic, trim the celery, seed the peppers, finely chop it all, and place in a large casserole pan on a medium heat with 1 tablespoon of oil and the bay leaves. Finely slice 1 chile and add to the pan, strip in the thyme leaves, then cook for 10 minutes, or until softened, stirring regularly.

Pour the black beans into the pan (juice and all), then half-fill each can with water, swirl around and pour into the pan. Bring to a boil, then simmer for around 30 minutes, or until thickened. At this point, use a potato masher to mash up half the soup, stirring it back through the rest to make it nice and creamy. Have a taste, and season to perfection. Crack the eggs directly into the soup to poach for around 6 minutes, or until cooked to your liking.

Meanwhile, finely chop the remaining chile (seed if you like) and the cilantro (stalks and all) on a board. Crumble over the feta, add a squeeze of lime juice, and keep chopping and mixing until nice and fine. Toast the tortillas directly over an open flame on the stove until scorched (or toast in a dry frying pan for 30 seconds). Serve the soup sprinkled with the salsa, bust up the eggs, and use the tortillas for dunking.

CALORIES	FAT	SAT FAT	PROTEIN	CARBS	SUGAR	SALT	FIBER	3 PORTIONS VEG & FRUIT
424kcal	14.5g	4g	22.1g	46.5g	9.9g	1.4g	17.4g	

FOUR SEASONS MINESTRONE
A CELEBRATION OF BEAUTIFUL VEGGIES

___ Each veg combo here guarantees we get all of our 5-a-day portions from just one serving— ___
what a lovely bowlful. Used minimally for seasoning, Parmesan is a good calcium source

EACH COMBO SERVES 4

1 HOUR 10 MINUTES

BASE RECIPE

2 onions

2 large carrots

2 stalks of celery

olive oil

2 fresh bay leaves

optional: 1 rasher of smoked
bacon

8 cups veg or chicken stock

1 x 15-oz can of cannellini beans

½ a Savoy or spring cabbage

5 oz dried spaghetti or fregola

2 oz Parmesan cheese

extra virgin olive oil

4 slices of whole-grain bread

Choose your **SEASONAL VEG**
combo: you want 1¾ lbs of extra
veg in total, so how you divvy
that up is your choice

BASE RECIPE Follow this method whatever the season, checking the notes below on how to celebrate each one. Peel the onions and carrots, trim the celery, then finely chop. Place in a large casserole pan on a medium-low heat with 1 tablespoon of olive oil, the bay leaves, and the smoky bacon (if using). Cook for 20 minutes, stirring occasionally. Pour in the stock, bring to a boil, and add the drained beans. Finely slice the cabbage leaves, removing the stalks, add to the pan, and simmer for 20 minutes. Smash up the spaghetti and add for a final 10 minutes. Loosen with a splash of boiling water, if needed, then taste and season to perfection. Serve with a grating of Parmesan, a few drips of extra virgin olive oil (new season's if possible), and bread for dunking.

SPRING VEG Trim asparagus and broccolini, then roughly chop. Add for the last 5 minutes, with fresh spinach and chopped fresh parsley.

SUMMER VEG Peel baby artichokes back to their pale leaves, then quarter each one and rub with lemon. Finely slice chard, then seed and dice tomatoes. Add with the spaghetti, adding fresh peas and fava beans at the end.

AUTUMN VEG Peel and seed squash and chop into ½-inch dice. Rehydrate ¾ oz of porcini mushrooms in boiling kettle water. Wipe fresh mushrooms clean and slice. Add the squash at the first stage of the base recipe, and drain, chop, and add the porcini, too. Add the fresh mushrooms with the spaghetti.

WINTER VEG Peel raw beets and chop into ½-inch dice. Discard cavolo nero and kale stalks, then finely slice the leaves. Add the beets at the first stage of the base recipe, adding the greens when you add the cabbage.

CALORIES	FAT	SAT FAT	PROTEIN	CARBS	SUGAR	SALT	FIBER	5 PORTIONS
559kcal	14.1g	4.3g	33.2g	73.4g	17.6g	0.9g	16.8g	VEG & FRUIT

THESE VALUES ARE AN AVERAGE OF THE FOUR RECIPES ABOVE

SUPER LEEK & POTATO SOUP
HERB, PARMESAN, & ALMOND TOASTS

I've taken family favorite leek and potato soup to the next level here by adding lots of lovely leafy kale, which—along with leeks—gives us vitamin B$_6$, helping us stay awake and alert

SERVES 4

40 MINUTES

14 oz leeks

olive oil

14 oz potatoes

6 cups veg or chicken stock

11 oz kale

½ a bunch of fresh mint (½ oz)

½ a bunch of fresh Italian
parsley (½ oz)

1½ oz Parmesan cheese

1 oz whole almonds

1 tablespoon white wine vinegar

extra virgin olive oil

4 small slices of whole-grain
bread (1⅓ oz each)

Trim and wash the leeks, then slice and place in a large casserole pan on a medium heat with 1 tablespoon of olive oil. Sweat for 10 minutes, stirring regularly, while you wash and finely slice the potatoes (leaving the skin on for extra nutritional benefit), then stir into the pan. Pour in the stock and boil hard for 15 minutes. Pick through the kale, discarding any tough stalks, and add to the pan for the last 5 minutes, pushing it down and covering with a lid.

Meanwhile, pick the mint leaves, then finely chop on a large board with the top leafy half of the parsley. Finely grate over the Parmesan, add the almonds, vinegar, and 1 tablespoon of extra virgin olive oil, then finely chop and mix together. Toast the bread, then divide up the herby mixture on top.

In batches, carefully pour the contents of the pan into a blender. Put the lid on securely, cover with a kitchen towel, and, holding it in place, blitz until super-smooth. Taste the soup and season to perfection. Divide between your bowls, and serve with those lovely loaded toasts on the side.

CALORIES	FAT	SAT FAT	PROTEIN	CARBS	SUGAR	SALT	FIBER	2 PORTIONS
374kcal	16.6g	3.5g	18.4g	37.3g	5.3g	0.7g	6.6g	VEG & FRUIT

MULLIGATAWNY
RICE, SPICE, LAMB, LENTILS, & VEG GALORE

Lovely lentils and chickpeas help to pack this super soup with fiber, plus chickpeas give us the mineral manganese, keeping the connective tissue in our bodies strong and healthy

SERVES 6

45 MINUTES

8 cups chicken stock

1½ cups brown rice

olive oil

8 oz lean ground lamb

1 heaping teaspoon curry powder

2 cloves of garlic

2½-inch piece of fresh gingerroot

1 bunch of fresh cilantro (1 oz)

2 onions

2 carrots

2 mixed-color peppers

¾ cup dried red split lentils

1 x 15-oz can of chickpeas

1 x 14-oz can of plum tomatoes

1 cup frozen peas

3 oz frozen chopped spinach

6 uncooked pappadams

6 tablespoons plain yogurt

Pour the stock into a large pan on a medium-high heat and, once boiling, cook the rice in it according to the package instructions. Meanwhile, place a large casserole pan on a medium-high heat with 1 tablespoon of oil, the lamb, and the curry powder. Stir frequently while you peel the garlic and ginger and finely chop with the cilantro stalks. Peel the onions and carrots, seed the peppers, and chop it all into ½-inch dice.

As soon as the lamb is really dark golden, stir the garlic, ginger, and cilantro stalks into the pan, followed 1 minute later by the chopped veg. Cook for 10 minutes, then stir in the lentils, chickpeas (juice and all), and canned tomatoes, breaking up the tomatoes with a wooden spoon. Stir in the stock and rice, then simmer for a further 10 minutes, or until thick and delicious, adding splashes of water to loosen, if needed. Stir in the frozen peas and spinach just before the end to warm through, then taste and season to perfection.

One by one, puff up your dry pappadams in the microwave for around 30 seconds each. Serve the soup in bowls, each with a dollop of yogurt, a sprinkling of cilantro leaves, and a pappadam on the side.

---------------------------------- *Veggie swap in* ----------------------------------
Make this dish veggie by swapping out the lamb for an equal
amount of chopped mushrooms, and switching to veg stock.

CALORIES	FAT	SAT FAT	PROTEIN	CARBS	SUGAR	SALT	FIBER	4 PORTIONS VEG & FRUIT
577kcal	14.2g	4.3g	35.2g	80.6g	13.3g	0.9g	10g	

KOREAN CHICKEN HOTPOT
NOODLES, MUSHROOMS, TOFU, & KIMCHEE

__ Although high in salt, when used in moderation (like anything!), fermented veg, like kimchee, __
are a source of probiotics, which are thought to keep our gut bacteria healthy and happy

SERVES 4

1 HOUR 10 MINUTES

5 oz shiitake mushrooms

2 large carrots

1 bunch of scallions

12 oz firm silken tofu

4 chicken thighs, skin on,
  bone in

4 cups chicken stock

1 teaspoon reduced-sodium
  soy sauce

2 teaspoons Korean chili paste
  or hot chili sauce

7 oz kimchee (find it in Asian
  supermarkets)

8 oz whole-wheat noodles

2 teaspoons sesame oil

2 teaspoons raw sesame seeds

1 lime

Wipe the mushrooms clean, trim the stalks, halve any larger mushrooms, then dry char in a large non-stick casserole pan on a medium heat for 5 minutes, or until dark golden and beautifully nutty, turning halfway. Meanwhile, peel the carrots and finely slice into rounds at an angle. Trim and roughly slice the scallions. Drain the tofu and chop into eight chunks.

Pull the skin off the chicken thighs and discard. Use the heel of a large knife to cut each thigh through the bone into three pieces by carefully and firmly tapping the knife with a rolling pin—this will add more flavor to the broth. Remove the mushrooms to a plate, and add the chicken and carrots to the pan. Cook for 10 minutes, stirring regularly. Pour in the stock, bring to a boil, then simmer for 20 minutes. Stir in the scallions, mushrooms, tofu, soy sauce, and chili paste and simmer for a final 20 minutes. Chop the kimchee and stir through just before serving (this means it isn't overexposed to heat, so will retain more of its nutritional benefit).

While the soup is simmering, cook the noodles according to the package instructions, then drain. Toss with the sesame oil and seeds, and divide between your bowls. Taste the broth, season to perfection, then squeeze in lime juice to add contrast. Divide between your hot noodle bowls, and enjoy.

CALORIES	FAT	SAT FAT	PROTEIN	CARBS	SUGAR	SALT	FIBER	2 PORTIONS
501kcal	13.2g	3.1g	37.8g	56.1g	8.1g	1.4g	5.7g	VEG & FRUIT

NAVAJO SOUP
SQUASH, BEANS, CORN, & FLATBREADS

Beans add color and provide us with a veggie source of protein in this recipe, plus they are a source of magnesium, which we need so that our muscles can function properly

SERVES 4

1 HOUR 10 MINUTES

1 butternut squash or pumpkin (2½ lbs)

1 onion

olive oil

6 cups veg or chicken stock

3½ oz polenta

2 x 15-oz cans of borlotti or pinto beans

1⅓ cups all-purpose whole-grain flour

¾ cup plain yogurt

1 bunch of fresh chives (1 oz)

Preheat the oven to 350°F. Clean the squash or pumpkin (there's no need to peel it), carefully halve it lengthways, then halve again into quarters and remove and discard the seeds. Place in a roasting pan, season with sea salt and black pepper, and roast for 1 hour, or until cooked through.

After 30 minutes, peel and finely chop the onion and place in a large casserole pan on a medium-low heat with 1 tablespoon of oil and a splash of water. Cook for 10 minutes, or until softened, stirring regularly. Pour the stock into the pan and bring to a boil, then whisk in the polenta (this will gradually thicken the soup, giving it a wonderful texture). Tip in the beans (juice and all), and leave to simmer away on the lowest heat until the squash is cooked.

Meanwhile, preheat a grill pan on a high heat. Mix the flour, yogurt, and a pinch of sea salt into a ball of dough. On a clean flour-dusted surface, divide the dough into four equal-sized pieces. One by one, roll each piece out nice and thinly, then dry grill until bar-marked on each side.

Chop up the soft, sweet squash, slice the chives, and stir both through the soup. Taste and season to perfection, adjust the consistency to your liking with splashes of water, then serve right away with the flatbreads for dunking.

CALORIES	FAT	SAT FAT	PROTEIN	CARBS	SUGAR	SALT	FIBER	2 PORTIONS VEG & FRUIT
554kcal	8.3g	2.2g	25.5g	97.6g	21.4g	1.2g	25.5g	

KITCHEN HACKS

Clever tricks and shortcuts to batch make,
helping you get ahead for future meals

PROPER CHICKEN NUGGETS
SWEET PAPRIKA & PARMESAN CRUMB

Using whole-grain bread instead of the usual white-bread coating means we are upping our fiber intake, and we've lowered the calories by baking rather than deep-frying these bad boys

MAKE 10 PORTIONS

30 MINUTES PREP
PLUS MARINATING

2 lbs boneless, skinless chicken breasts

2 cloves of garlic

1 level teaspoon sweet smoked paprika

1 heaping tablespoon Greek yogurt

1 large egg

1 lemon

8 oz whole-grain bread

1¾ oz Parmesan cheese

olive oil

Start by cutting the chicken breasts into nugget-sized portions. The easiest way to do this is to use your scales to help you get it right the first time—you want each nugget to be just over 1 oz, then visually that will give you a guide for the rest. Cut up all the chicken, putting it on a tray as you go.

To make the marinade, crush the unpeeled garlic cloves through a garlic crusher over the chicken. Add the paprika, yogurt, egg, and a good pinch of sea salt and black pepper. Finely grate over the lemon zest and squeeze over all the juice, then use your clean hands to massage all that flavor into the meat. Cover and marinate in the fridge for at least 1 hour, or overnight.

Tear the bread into a food processor, finely grate in the Parmesan, add 2 tablespoons of oil, and whiz until you have fine bread crumbs, then tip into a large shallow tray (this is probably more bread than you need, but it's easier to work with—simply discard whatever's left). Working in batches, use two forks to transfer the pieces of chicken into the crumbs, using the forks to gently flick crumbs over each piece of chicken so it's well coated. Transfer the nuggets to a deep pan lined with parchment paper, layering them up between sheets of paper as you go. Cook right away or freeze in the pan—once frozen, you can pop them into a tub or sandwich bags for easier storage.

To cook, place however many nuggets you need on a rack in a roasting pan in a preheated oven at 350°F for 15 to 20 minutes, or until golden and cooked through.

CALORIES	FAT	SAT FAT	PROTEIN	CARBS	SUGAR	SALT	FIBER
230kcal	7.8g	2.4g	29.4g	10g	0.9g	0.7g	1.6g

CHICKEN NUGGETS
X 10 PORTIONS
14/02/16

BATCH GROUND MEAT RAGÙ
LOADSA VEG, BEANS, & SUN-DRIED TOMATOES

Bulking out ground meat with beans is a great habit to get into, as it means we get extra protein without extra saturated fat from the meat, plus beans give us gut-friendly fiber—win win!

MAKES 10 PORTIONS
(6.5 LBS)

1 HOUR 50 MINUTES

2 rashers of smoked bacon

olive oil

2 lbs lean ground beef

2 x 15-oz cans of beans, such as
adzuki, cannellini, pinto

2 sprigs of fresh rosemary

2 fresh bay leaves

optional: Chianti

2 large onions

2 large carrots

1 celery heart

1 x 8½-oz jar of sun-dried
tomatoes in oil

2 tablespoons balsamic vinegar

2 x 14-oz cans of plum tomatoes

This is a really convenient, nutritious standby to have in the fridge or freezer, which can easily be taken lots of ways—serve simply with pasta, hunks of bread, or a baked potato, or use in cottage pie, lasagne, cannelloni, and chili.

Finely slice the bacon and place in a large casserole pan on a medium-high heat with 1 tablespoon of oil. Once golden, stir in the ground meat, breaking it up with a wooden spoon. Drain and add the beans, pick, finely chop, and add the rosemary leaves, along with the bay, then cook it all for 20 minutes, or until dark golden, stirring regularly. Any time it starts to catch at the bottom of the pan, simply add a splash of wine (if using) or water to pick up all those nice, sticky bits. Preheat the oven to 400°F.

Peel the onions and carrots, trim the celery, then finely chop it all (by hand or in a food processor). Stir into the pan and cook for another 15 minutes. Tip the contents of the sun-dried tomato jar into a blender, add the balsamic, and blitz until smooth. Stir 2 tablespoons into the pan, then decant the rest back into the jar, popping it into the fridge for another day—it will be delicious brushed onto meat, fish, or veg before roasting or grilling, or used on crostini.

Pour the canned tomatoes into the pan, along with 2 cans' worth of water. Mix well, bring to a boil, then pop into the oven uncovered for 1 hour, or until thick and reduced. Taste, season to perfection, and cool. Once cool, divide between containers or bags, and pop portions into the fridge or freezer until needed.

CALORIES	FAT	SAT FAT	PROTEIN	CARBS	SUGAR	SALT	FIBER	2 PORTIONS VEG & FRUIT
250kcal	9g	3g	25.8g	15.2g	7g	0.5g	5g	

JUMBO FISH FINGERS
GOLDEN CRISPY BREAD CRUMBS

The perfect family favorite to have in the freezer, fish, especially salmon, is packed with omega-3 fatty acids, which are essential for keeping our blood cholesterol healthy

MAKES 10 PORTIONS
25 MINUTES PREP

1 x 2½ lbs side of salmon,
   skin off, pin-boned

2 large eggs

1 teaspoon sweet smoked paprika

8 oz whole-grain bread

1 oz Cheddar cheese

extra virgin olive oil

Did you know?

Sides of salmon are often on sale—it's simply one of the realities of the fish farming industry that due to variations in supply and demand, there'll be surpluses. So when you see salmon on sale—take action and take advantage of that great value!

Something as humble and everyday as a fish finger can be made even more nutritious if you make your own, and even better, you can go jumbo in size! I like to use salmon but, of course, white fish works well, too.

Cut the fish into 10 x 4-oz portions. The nature of the shape of the salmon side means that they won't be uniform in size, but that's all part of their charm. I tend to cut the side lengthways about 1¼ inch thick, then into chunks from that.

In a shallow bowl, whisk the eggs with the paprika and a pinch of sea salt and black pepper. Tear the bread into a food processor, grate in the cheese, add 2 tablespoons of oil, and whiz until you have bread crumbs, then tip into a tray (this is probably more bread than you need, but it is easier to work with—simply discard whatever's left). Coat each fish portion in the egg mixture, let any excess drip off, then turn in the bread crumbs until well coated all over. Transfer to a pan lined with parchment paper, layering them up between sheets of paper until they're all coated. Cook right away or freeze in the pan—once frozen, you can pop them into a container or sandwich bags for easier storage.

To cook, place however many jumbo fish fingers you need on a roasting pan and cook in a preheated oven at 400°F for 15 minutes from fresh, or 20 minutes from frozen, or until golden and cooked through.

CALORIES	FAT	SAT FAT	PROTEIN	CARBS	SUGAR	SALT	FIBER
325kcal	18.6g	3.8g	29.1g	9.5g	0.6g	0.5g	1.6g

WEEKLY POACHED CHICKEN
INCREDIBLE FLAVORSOME STOCK

— Chicken gives us selenium, which we need for lots of functions, from making sure our immune systems are ticking over nicely to keeping our hair and nails strong and healthy —

STOCK: 14 CUPS
CHICKEN: 8 PORTIONS
3 HOURS

1 x 4 lbs whole chicken

2 fresh bay leaves

1 bunch of fresh Italian
    parsley (1 oz)

1 leek

1 carrot

1 stalk of celery

1 onion

extra virgin olive oil

At home, I don't want to spend all day boiling bones to make stock. However, I'm really happy to make tasty stock, like in this recipe, if I'm poaching tender chicken at the same time, creating the base for a few lunches and dinners throughout that week. This is a process I tend to do every weekend.

So, get your biggest stock pot and sit the whole chicken inside it. Add the bay, parsley, and a good pinch of sea salt and black pepper. Wash and roughly chop the leek, carrot, and celery, then peel and quarter the onion. Chuck it all into the pan and cover with 16 cups of water, making sure the chicken is submerged. Bring to a simmer on a medium heat, then cook for 1 hour 30 minutes, turning occasionally. Avoid boiling it, so the meat stays tender.

Use tongs to carefully remove the chicken to a large bowl to cool a little, leaving the stock on the heat for another 1 hour 30 minutes to intensify that flavor. Once the chicken is cool enough to handle, wear rubber gloves or use tongs to pull all the meat off the carcass, discarding the skin as you go, and chucking the bones back into the stock for added flavor. Toss the meat with 1 tablespoon of oil, and once completely cool, cover and pop into the fridge for up to 3 days, ready to be used in salads, sandwiches, and stir-fries.

Sieve the stock, discarding the contents of the sieve. Cool and place in the fridge, where it will set as jelly and be good for at least 1 week, or bag it up and freeze it. Of course, you can always cook extra veg in the stock, and make yourself a hearty bowl of chicken and veg broth to enjoy that day—I find this useful if I've got the family coming and going, as it sits quite happily on the stove over the lowest heat, ready to portion up as you need it.

CALORIES	FAT	SAT FAT	PROTEIN	CARBS	SUGAR	SALT	FIBER
175kcal	8.3g	2.1g	24.7g	0.4g	0.3g	0.4g	0g

SUPER-QUICK BATCH PESTO
NUTS, PARMESAN, & LOADSA BASIL

Using creamy almonds in this pesto gives us protein, as well as lots of other lovely nutrients, including a big hit of vitamin E, which we need to protect our cells from damage

7 oz Parmesan cheese

2 big bunches of fresh basil
(2 oz each)

2 cloves of garlic

3½ oz pine nuts

3½ oz blanched almonds

1 lemon

6 tablespoons + 2 teaspoons
extra virgin olive oil

Making pesto is such an easy thing to do, you'll wonder why you've never gotten into the habit of doing it from scratch before. The quantities I've given you here mean you can utilize whole packages of Parmesan and nuts, and the method is so simple anyone can do it. This is one of those incredible recipes where minimum effort gives you maximum flavor, every time.

Break the Parmesan into a food processor (discarding the rind). Rip in the leafy basil, discarding only the tougher base of the stalks. Peel and add the garlic, and tip in the pine nuts and almonds. Finely grate in the lemon zest, squeeze in all the juice, and pour in the oil. Blitz until fairly fine in consistency.

The fresh pesto will keep well in the fridge for up to 3 days, and it freezes brilliantly. The easiest thing to do is roll the pesto up in parchment paper to make a log, then scrunch the ends like a cracker. Pop into the freezer for 2 hours, then, before it gets too hard, remove, unwrap, and slice into the appropriate number of portions. Reshape, reroll, and rewrap, then pop it back into the freezer—it'll be good for at least 3 months. To use from frozen, simply defrost overnight in the fridge, or whack it straight into a pan to melt.

CALORIES	FAT	SAT FAT	PROTEIN	CARBS	SUGAR	SALT	FIBER
188kcal	17.3g	3.8g	7g	1.3g	0.7g	0.2g	0g

7-VEG TOMATO SAUCE
PACKED WITH HIDDEN GOODNESS

— Jam-packed with nutritious veg, this has to be one of the easiest ways to get extra
veggie portions into our diet, as well as all sorts of brilliant micronutrients —

MAKES 14 TO 16 CUPS

1 HOUR

2 small onions

2 small leeks

2 stalks of celery

2 carrots

2 zucchini

2 red peppers

½ a butternut squash (1¼ lbs)

2 cloves of garlic

olive oil

2 teaspoons dried oregano

4 x 14-oz cans of plum tomatoes

Start with your veg prep—you can either do this by hand (which is a great way to practice your knife skills) or, in batches, rattle it all through a food processor. Peel the onions, wash and trim the leeks, celery, carrots, and zucchini, seed the peppers and squash (there's no need to peel it), then finely chop it all. Peel the garlic and finely chop by hand.

Put a super-large pan on a medium heat with 2 tablespoons of oil. Add the garlic and oregano, fry for 1 minute, then add all the prepped veg. Cook with the lid on for 25 minutes, or until the veg are soft but not colored, stirring regularly. Pour in the canned tomatoes, breaking them up with a wooden spoon, then just under half-fill each can with water, swirl around and pour into the pan. Simmer for 25 minutes, or until the sauce has reduced. Leave to cool a little, then blitz until smooth, taste, and season to perfection.

Freezer friendly

Divide up this batch recipe and freeze for future meals, from cheat's pizzetta (see page 94) to simple pastas (see pages 54–6). In recipes using more than one can of tomatoes, try swapping out one can for a can's worth of this sauce, for an extra boost.

Embrace the seasons

It's always nice to celebrate the changing seasons and add extra veg into the mix, depending on what's available and at its best.

CALORIES	FAT	SAT FAT	PROTEIN	CARBS	SUGAR	SALT	FIBER
32kcal	1g	0.1g	1.3g	4.8g	3.6g	0.1g	1g

THESE VALUES ARE BASED ON 100ML OF SAUCE

FREEZER TIPS

* Label and date bags clearly so you
  can rotate food efficiently.
* If food has thawed, do not refreeze.
  Use as soon as possible.
* Cook vegetables from frozen.
* Freeze food in meal size portions
  for convenience and to avoid waste.

DATE
14/02/16
CONTENTS
7 - VEG
SAUCE

CURRY PASTES
KORMA, JALFREZI, & THAI GREEN

— Even when used in small amounts, all these nutrient-dense spices and seeds are beneficial. —
For example, cumin, mustard, coriander, and fenugreek seeds are all mega-high in iron

EACH PASTE MAKES 10 PORTIONS

KORMA Toast **2 teaspoons of cumin seeds** and **1 teaspoon of coriander seeds** in a dry frying pan for 2 minutes, then tip into a food processor. Peel and add **2 cloves of garlic** and a **2-inch piece of fresh gingerroot**, along with **1 teaspoon of garam masala**, ½ a teaspoon of sea salt, **2 tablespoons of peanut oil, 1 tablespoon of tomato purée, 2 fresh green chiles, 3 tablespoons of unsweetened desiccated coconut, 2 tablespoons of ground almonds**, and ½ **a bunch of fresh cilantro (½ oz)**. Squeeze in the juice of ½ **a lemon** and blitz to a paste, scraping down the sides halfway.

JALFREZI Toast **2 teaspoons of cumin seeds** and **1 teaspoon each of coriander seeds, fenugreek seeds, and black mustard seeds** in a dry frying pan for 2 minutes, then tip into a food processor. Peel and add **2 cloves of garlic** and a **2-inch piece of fresh gingerroot**, along with **1 teaspoon of ground turmeric**, ½ a teaspoon of sea salt, **2 tablespoons of peanut oil, 2 tablespoons of tomato purée, 1 fresh red chile**, and ½ **a bunch of fresh cilantro (½ oz)**. Squeeze in the juice of ½ **a lemon** and blitz to a paste, scraping down the sides halfway.

THAI GREEN Toast **1 teaspoon of cumin seeds** in a dry frying pan for 2 minutes, then tip into a food processor. Peel and add **2 cloves of garlic, 2 shallots**, and a **2-inch piece of fresh gingerroot**, along with **4 kaffir lime leaves, 2 tablespoons of peanut oil, 2 tablespoons of fish sauce, 4 fresh green chiles, 2 tablespoons of unsweetened desiccated coconut**, and **1 bunch of fresh cilantro (1 oz)**. Bash **2 stalks of lemongrass**, remove and discard the outer layer, then snap into the processor, squeeze in the juice of ½ **a lime**, and blitz to a paste, scraping down the sides halfway.

TO STORE Line the base of an egg carton with plastic wrap, place 1 heaping tablespoon of paste in five of the wells, cover with plastic wrap, and freeze. Each ball of paste is equivalent to 2 portions.

CALORIES	FAT	SAT FAT	PROTEIN	CARBS	SUGAR	SALT	FIBER
41kcal	3.8g	1g	1g	1.4g	0.8g	0.3g	0.5g

THESE VALUES ARE AN AVERAGE OF THE THREE RECIPES ABOVE

AMAZING STEWED ORCHARD FRUIT & JAM
APPLES & PEARS, BAY, ORANGE, & VANILLA

All fruit contains natural sugar, but most jams have a load of added sugar, too—this recipe gives you a super-jammy result, with zero added sugar, plus nutrients from the fruit

MAKES 16 PORTIONS
2 HOURS 30 MINUTES

2 lbs crisp eating apples

2 lbs pears

3 oranges

1 fresh bay leaf

1 pinch of ground cinnamon

1 vanilla bean

Every week we make this at home. You can simply stew the fruit, or you can cook it super low and slow and turn it into fruit jam—I tend to do half and half.

Peel and core the apples and pears and cut into quarters, chucking them into a large non-stick casserole pan as you go. When they're in season, it's always joyful to add a handful of blackberries or raspberries, too. Squeeze over all the orange juice, add a splash of water, the bay leaf and cinnamon, then halve the vanilla bean lengthways, scrape out the seeds and add both bean and seeds to the pan. Place on a medium-low heat with a lid on for 40 minutes, or until the fruit is soft and nicely stewed, stirring occasionally.

At this point, you can choose to leave it as is, letting it cool, then popping it into the fridge ready to enjoy on oatmeal, yogurt, or granola, to put into smoothies, to enjoy as a snack, or even to add sweetness to stews and gravies. Or, you can turn it into jam—or what is often called a fruit butter. Simply leave it on a super-low heat with the lid off for around another 1 hour 20 minutes, mashing occasionally to help it along, until dark, thick, and spreadable. It's reliable, so you can pretty much leave it ticking away. Once cool, decant into a jar, keep in the fridge, and it will be an absolute treat spread on whole-grain toast, oat crackers, crumpets, or waffles. Enjoy.

CALORIES	FAT	SAT FAT	PROTEIN	CARBS	SUGAR	SALT	FIBER	1 PORTION VEG & FRUIT
57kcal	0.2g	0g	0.6g	14.2g	14g	0g	2.6g	

FRUIT POPSICLES
LOADS OF SUPER-FUN INSPIRATION

Celebrating the natural sweetness of fruit, these colorful popsicles avoid the added sugars we find in most store-bought versions, providing a delicious, nutritious snack or dessert

After dinner, my kids always ask for something sweet, and along with fruit and yogurt, one of the staples we always have in stock is homemade popsicles. A lot of desserts flash red on the nutritional scale and are wolfed down in a minute, but these beauties are guaranteed to keep the kids quiet for 8 minutes straight, as well as getting some fruit into them. They're super-simple to make, you can get the kids involved putting them together, and my lot love them, me and Jools included! Below are our favorite combos, but feel free to make up your own and vary the quantities to suit your molds—just make sure you dilute any straight fruit juices with water or coconut water, and give your concoctions a taste before freezing to check the balance of fruity flavors.

1. In a blender, blitz **fresh or frozen chunks of mango** with some finely grated **lime** zest, a nice squeeze of lime juice, and some **coconut water**, then divide between popsicle molds and freeze.

2. Halve wrinkly **passion fruit**, then scoop out and divide the seeds between popsicle molds. Squeeze **clementine** juice into a pitcher, dilute with water, then divide between the molds and freeze.

3. Peel **watermelon**, peel and core **crisp eating apples**, blitz in a food processor with a little hum of finely grated peeled **fresh gingerroot**, then divide between popsicle molds and freeze (or keep separate, freezing in fruity layers).

4. Peel and tear **ripe bananas** into a blender, add a little **quality cocoa powder** and some **almond milk**, blitz until smooth, then divide between popsicle molds and freeze (1 banana, 1 teaspoon of cocoa, a scant 1 cup of milk is good).

5. Decant **canned pineapple chunks** (juice and all), into a blender with a few freshly picked **mint leaves**, add some **coconut water**, blitz until super-smooth, then divide between popsicle molds and freeze.

6. Pour **unsweetened apple juice** into a blender with an equal amount of water. Add **blackberries**, **blueberries**, and a **pinch of ground cinnamon**, blitz until smooth, then divide between popsicle molds and freeze.

7. Drain **canned lychees**, peel and seed **honeydew melon**, blitz both in a blender with finely grated **lime** zest and a squeeze of lime juice until smooth, then divide between popsicle molds and freeze.

HEALTH & HAPPINESS

Tips, tricks, and advice on food, nutrition, and well-being to help you and your family live well

My super-food philosophy
ENERGY & THE BALANCED PLATE

Balance is absolutely key. If you can balance your plate right and keep your portion control in check—which I've done for you with all the recipes in this book—you can be confident that you're giving yourself, and your family, a really great start on the path to good health.

You don't have to be spot-on every day—just try to get your balance right across the week. If you eat meat and fish, as a general guide for main meals you're looking at at least two portions of fish a week, one of which should be oily (such as salmon, trout, or mackerel), then splitting the rest of the week's main meals between brilliant meat-free plant-based meals, some poultry, and a little red meat. An all-vegetarian diet can be perfectly healthy, too.

How to balance your plate

THE FIVE FOOD GROUPS (UK)	PROPORTION OF YOUR PLATE
Vegetables and fruit	Just over one-third (around 40%)
Starchy carbohydrates (bread, rice, potatoes, pasta)	Just over one-third (around 40%)
Protein (meat, fish, eggs, beans, other non-dairy sources)	Around one-eighth (just over 10%)
Dairy foods, milk, and dairy alternatives	Around one-eighth (just under 10%)
Unsaturated fats (such as oils)	Use in small amounts
And don't forget to drink plenty of water, too—read more on page 258	

THE RECIPE STRUCTURE IN THIS BOOK

× All the main meals, which can be used for lunch or dinner interchangeably, are 600 calories or less per portion and contain 6g or less of saturated fat and 1.5g or less of salt. Each of these meals contains at least 2 portions of veg and fruit, and this is clearly signposted on each recipe page to help you out

× Breakfasts are less than 400 calories per portion and contain less than 4g of saturated fat and 1.5g of salt

× This framework allows for a few energy-boosting snacks a day, with some calories left for drinks

× The Kitchen Hacks chapter is about meal elements you can have in the bag ready to go, so remember the balanced plate philosophy when you use those

WHAT DOES THAT MEAN IN REAL LIFE?

Energy—in the form of calories—is essential to life. We need energy to move, so that our organs function, and for growth, repair, and development. Of course, everyone is different, so our requirements vary, but a lot of research has gone into energy balance, so these UK guideline figures are a really useful place to start:

AGE	FEMALE CALORIES PER DAY	MALE CALORIES PER DAY
11 and over	2000	2500
10	1936	2032
9	1721	1840
8	1625	1745
7	1530	1649
6	1482	1577
5	1362	1482
4	1291	1386

Just remember that what we eat always needs to be considered in relation to gender, age, build, lifestyle, and activity levels, so use your common sense and tweak meals according to your family's needs. The good news is that all food and drinks can be eaten and drunk in moderation as part of a healthy, balanced diet, so we don't have to completely give up anything that we really enjoy, unless we're advised to do so by a doctor or dietitian. Listen to your body and try to ensure you achieve a balance between enjoying food and leading a physically active life.

ENERGY INTAKE & EXPENDITURE

We get our energy from food and drink, by breaking down the fat, carbohydrates, protein, and fiber they contain. As already mentioned, energy requirements vary from person to person. As well as age, build, lifestyle, and activity levels, they're determined by our genes, gender, weight, and even the climate we live in. All of these factors need to be balanced with the food and drink we consume, and the additional energy we use, otherwise we will lose or gain weight.

It's completely natural for our weight to fluctuate a little bit from week to week, and year to year, but generally we should try to maintain a consistent weight and this is best achieved through a healthy, balanced diet. Current guidelines recommend that we consume about 20% of our energy at breakfast, 30% each at lunch and dinner, with the remaining 20% for snacks and drinks. This is the framework I've stuck to in this book, so you can pick and choose freely among the chapters, knowing you are in a good place to achieve your energy requirements for the day.

It's worth noting that some studies are now emerging that suggest it could be beneficial to our health to eat dinner earlier in the evening, creating more of a fast between dinner and breakfast the following day. These studies are based on what happens to our metabolisms and our body clocks (known as our circadian rhythm) throughout the day, and the evidence suggests that as the day goes on, our bodies process food differently. So making the effort to eat dinner a little bit earlier may help to make us healthier and happier!

Live well

TOP TIPS FROM EVERYDAY SUPER FOOD

When I was writing my last book, *Everyday Super Food*, I was also studying for my nutrition diploma, and had the privilege of meeting lots of incredible scientists, professors, and experts in their field in order to share the most useful and accessible info out there with you. It was all fascinating stuff, so I wanted to share a super-short summary here, in bite-sized nuggets, for you to digest. Happy reading.

— Eat breakfast —

It's so important in setting you up for the day. Not only will it fill you up and prevent you snacking on foods high in fat/sugar, it can kick you off with a lovely boost of micronutrients, too. For loads of super-delicious ideas to get you excited, see pages 10–41.

TRADE UP YOUR CARBS

Starchy carbs are wonderful—they make us feel happy, satisfied, and energetic, and provide a large proportion of the energy we need to move our bodies, and the fuel our organs need to function. Choose fiber-rich whole-grain and whole-wheat varieties when you can, which take longer to break down, are slow-releasing, and give us a more sustained level of energy, also helping us feel fuller for longer.

EMBRACE VEG & FRUIT

To live a good, healthy life, veg and fruit need to be right at the heart of your diet. Eat the rainbow, mixing up your choices with the seasons and enjoying as wide a variety as possible. We should all be aiming for at least five 3-oz portions of fresh, frozen, or canned veg and fruit every day of the week, ideally more. You can also count one 1-oz portion of dried fruit per day, or 3 oz of beans or pulses.

CHOOSE ORGANIC

Whenever you can, trade up, for your own health and for the good of the planet. I'm sure most of us will agree that putting natural ingredients into our bodies is only going to be a positive thing. Plus, if we all start to readdress what we buy, cook, and eat, gradually buying better and wasting less, that's only going to help to move our food system forward in a positive and more sustainable way.

Stay hydrated

To be the very best you can be, staying hydrated is absolutely key. After all, water is essential to life! Read more on page 258.

Control your protein intake

While protein is an integral part of our diet, it does, like everything else, need to be eaten in the right amounts. Think of protein as the building blocks of our bodies—it's used for everything that's important to how we grow, repair, feel, break down and absorb things, and how we fight disease and infections. Generally, the optimal amount for women aged 19–50 is 45g per day, with 55g for men in the same age bracket, then 28g for children aged 7–10, and 20g for children aged 4–6.

— Eat more fiber —

Found mainly in plant-based foods, fiber is also classed as a carbohydrate. Most of us need to up our fiber intake—read why on page 252.

DON'T BE AFRAID OF FAT

Of course, fat consumption needs to be controlled, but a healthy diet does require good fats, so choose unsaturated sources where you can, such as olive and liquid vegetable oils, nuts, seeds, avocado, and omega-3-rich oily fish. Healthy fats give us energy and help us to store it, provide insulation and protection for our internal organs, supply essential fatty acids, and help us absorb fat-soluble vitamins and other nutrients.

Get enough sleep

It sounds simple, but getting enough sleep is absolutely essential, and really is one of the biggest contributors to good health, giving our bodies that crucial time they need to grow, heal, and repair. Less than six hours and more than nine over a sustained period can increase our risk of developing an illness, so it's definitely worth spending the time to get this right.

INCLUDE DAIRY IN YOUR MEALS

Dairy foods, milk, and dairy alternatives (such as fortified almond or oat milk) offer us an amazing array of nutrients. Just remember that it's organic milk, yogurt, and small amounts of cheese, rather than butter and cream, that we should generally be favoring as the portion of dairy in our meals.

— Get moving —

Movement is incredibly important, and being active should be a natural habit in all aspects of daily life—let's all challenge ourselves to be more naturally active each day and quite simply to move a bit more!

+ HAVE A 3-DAY BREAK FROM BOOZE +

And do this every week to give your liver a break. Regardless of quality, alcohol, as far as your body is concerned, is not nutritious and is toxic, and it's very high in calories, too. It's also been responsible for some of the worst behavior on the planet! But I do love it—just please be responsible.

The genius of chewing
YOUR STOMACH DOESN'T HAVE TEETH

First up, guys, let's get one thing straight: your stomach doesn't have teeth! I know that sounds obvious, but it seems to be a modern-day phenomenon that people eat on the fly and almost breathe in their food rather than chewing and savoring it. So, let me give you some nice geeky information about how chewing can be the profound beginning to not overeating, enjoying food more, and ensuring we are able to absorb and benefit from all the nutrients and goodness in the food we eat. How cool is that—with every meal we all have the power to make a massive impact on our health.

WHAT HAPPENS WHEN WE CHEW

The digestion process starts in the mouth. When we chew food, it's lubricated by saliva, and our teeth shear through it, making it easier to digest and swallow. Chewing also produces digestive enzymes that mean we can break down our food properly, so it's easier to digest as it moves through our gut (see page 250) on the journey to our stomach, as well as helping us to extract the maximum amount of nutrients.

At the same time, the very act of chewing acts as a signal to our bodies that food is about to begin that journey. If we don't chew our food properly, then not only are our bodies underprepared for what's coming, we are also making our system work much harder in order to digest food, slowing that process right down.

OPTIMUM CHEWING

It's hard to be specific but, for sure, most of us could do with chewing just that little bit more. There isn't currently any definitive evidence on how much we should chew each bite of food, but it's looking like around 20 chews per bite might turn out to be the average optimum amount. However, it's really important not to get fixated on it, as one thing studies so far have definitely shown is that focusing on a specific number of chews can lead to irritability and fatigue, thus meaning we don't get the same enjoyment from our food. Also, different foods take a different number of chews to break down, so it's near impossible to prescribe the perfect amount—just chew more!

ALL ABOUT APPETITE

Let me try to explain the difference between appetite and hunger. We know that we need to eat to survive, in order to gain energy for everything we do. Our bodies are able to physiologically react to our needs, such as low blood sugar levels, sending a message to our brain that we need to eat in order to stay alive—this feeling is called hunger. Appetite, however, is our desire for food— it's the sensation of wanting food after the process of eating has begun, which means we can sustain our food intake. As satiation—the feeling of becoming full or satisfied—develops, our appetite lessens. Appetite is controlled by our brain, and reacts to signals from the gut to help us recognize when we're full. It's sensory, so even seeing or smelling food can make it kick in.

As we eat, the feeling of satiation develops—the more we chew something, the more it is exposed to the sensory receptors in our mouth, in turn increasing satiation. A good example I was told recently is the comparison between drinking a glass of apple juice and eating an apple. The first can be done in seconds, barely engaging our sensory receptors, whereas the latter takes a few minutes (even if you are super-hungry!). Based on what we've learnt, it makes sense that the process of eating an apple—and the time it takes—is much more likely to satisfy our hunger.

So, as I'm sure you can guess, if we rush our food, which we so often do, our bodies can't keep up and will be one step behind us, as it takes a while for our stomach to signal to our brain that we're full, so we're likely to eat more than we need. Taking our time and enjoying our food is not only good for our gut health, it can help us to manage our portion control, in turn preventing overeating and potential weight gain. Win win.

Interestingly, all foods can influence appetite if we like them. This is why we always seem to be able to eat a dessert, even when we feel full. It's a proper scientific phenomenon! It's called sensory specific satiety, and explains why once we start eating something sweet that we love, we suddenly seem able to fit it all in. So just be mindful of that, especially if you're keeping an eye on your weight—we love treats, but they should be just that, treats, and only enjoyed occasionally.

GIVING MORE TIME TO MEALTIMES

It's great to learn about chewing and the benefits it has, but I know when it comes to planning a meal, especially for the family, there can be loads of things to think about. I don't want to add one more to the pile, but we do have to eat, so let's try to make mealtimes the best they can be. I've always been a massive advocate of sitting down at the table to enjoy a good meal, whether you're with family or friends, or even on your own, so that you can savor each mouthful and take your time over the food you're eating, rather than rushing it. So in my mind, a really simple way to have a positive impact on your chewing habits is to sit down with other people more often—by default this will stimulate conversation, slowing down the rate you're eating, increasing your enjoyment, and in turn preventing overeating. If you're eating on your own, taking the time to enjoy a meal still applies—try to remove yourself from distractions like TV and allow yourself to focus on the food in front of you, actually tasting and savoring each mouthful, and slowing down that whole mealtime process.

And this doesn't just apply to the meals we eat at home. I know it can be hard sometimes to take time out for lunch when you're at work, especially if the culture where you are means that taking a lunch break is uncommon. But, whenever you can, try to get away from your desk or the environment you work in, and take the time to sit somewhere and savor your food. Just 20 minutes will do it, if that's all you can spare, and as well as helping your digestive system, it will give you time to pause, reflect, and unwind, hopefully revitalizing you for the rest of the day!

Healthy gut, happy body
THE NEXT BIG THING IN HEALTH

Everyone is familiar with the phrase "You are what you eat," but actually, you are what you absorb, and this is where good gut health comes into play. The gut is our gastrointestinal tract, basically the long tube that starts at the mouth and ends at the anus. It's integral to our overall health, affecting everything from our metabolism to our immune system function and even our mood. Yes, it involves our digestive system and talking about how it all works down there, but we shouldn't feel shy about discussing it. It looks like balancing our gut health is going to be a big topic in the next decade—there's loads of research being undertaken, and new findings are emerging all the time.

GUT MICROBIOTA

Microbiota is the name given to the trillions of microorganisms or bacteria living in our gut, made up from thousands of different species. It's always been thought that microorganisms make up over 90% of our cells, but new research has just shown that we actually have an equal amount of microorganisms and other cells (red blood, muscle, and fat). Two-thirds of our gut microbiota is completely unique to us, similar to DNA.

When we're in our mother's womb our gut is sterile, meaning it's completely free from these bacteria. During labor we acquire gut microbes from our mum's body, as well as from the environment we're born in and the air around us. Our microbiota is influenced by what we're fed as a baby—breast milk from a mum who has a healthy balanced diet is really beneficial here—and changes up to the age of about 3 years old, when it starts to stabilize. So, those early years can be really important to our future gut health.

WHAT GUT MICROBIOTA DOES

When we feed our gut microbiota it increases in numbers, helping us to have a happy gut. As well as helping us to maintain a healthy digestive system, it:

× Helps us to break down foods that we cannot digest, specifically fiber, into energy that we can actually use

× Helps our immune system to fight infection and helps to prevent harmful bacteria from transferring into our bloodstream

× Helps with the production of some vitamins, such as:

- Vitamin B_{12}—for healthy metabolism, immune and nervous system function, and red blood cell formation, keeping us awake and alert

- Vitamin K—for strong healthy bones (see page 255) and good blood clotting

- Folate—preventing tiredness

PROBIOTICS VS. PREBIOTICS

Probiotics can be really helpful and are readily available in various forms on the shelves of our supermarkets, but it's looking like prebiotics are the holy grail. And I have to tell you, the best prebiotic going is a healthy, balanced diet. Let me explain what the differences between them are, and what we currently know.

PROBIOTICS

Probiotics are live bacteria that are commonly known to aid gut health, and are often referred to as "friendly bacteria." Currently there aren't actually any health claims that can be made about probiotics, but they are thought to help restore the natural balance in our gut, especially after a course of antibiotics, which can often disrupt our gut microbiota.

There are loads of different types of probiotics, the most common being lactobacillus and bifidobacterium, which you might have seen on packaging. These different probiotics can help with different things, though it's not yet clear which ones are good at which things! Benefits include easing the symptoms of irritable bowel syndrome (IBS), aiding digestion, and improving our immune response.

Probiotics are naturally present in a few foods, namely plain yogurt, and fermented foods such as kimchee and sauerkraut (the latter are beneficial, but should be enjoyed in small amounts due to their high salt content). You can also take probiotics in the form of yogurt drinks, some of which contain up to billions per milliliter (just be wary of added sugars), and as tablets, capsules, and powder. What's not clear, when it comes to these products, is whether they contain enough bacteria to have an impact, or whether the bacteria can survive the digestive process long enough to make it down to your lower gut (the colon) and do its thing. Emerging research is suggesting that small microcapsule probiotics seem to stand the best chance of holding up against stomach acid and surviving that journey to the colon, so look out for more on this.

The key is to vary the way you top up your probiotics, increasing your chance of feeling the benefits.

PREBIOTICS

Eating a diet naturally rich in prebiotics looks like it can change our gut environment for the better. Prebiotics are naturally found in some plant fibers, the most common being oligosaccharides, such as inulin. This is found in foods such as bananas, onions, garlic, asparagus, leeks, artichokes, endive, and whole grains, particularly oats. As you'll see, these are fairly common ingredients, so if you can start including them in your diet more regularly, that's only going to be a good thing.

We can't digest these plant fibers but our gut microbiota can, and it flourishes on them, causing it to grow and multiply. Our gut microbiota is also able to ferment some other fibers that we can't digest, turning them into short chain fatty acids. These acids are able to influence our gut environment by lowering the pH level, in turn keeping our gut healthy and increasing the amount of nutrients we can utilize from our food.

Why fiber is cool
HOW TO UP YOUR INTAKE

What you'll learn on this page is just how simple it is to up your fiber intake—I genuinely believe it is one of the easiest areas of our diets we can improve on. As adults, we should be aiming for about 30g of fiber each day, but here in the UK on average we're well under 20g a day. Let's fix that!

WHY WE NEED FIBER

Fiber is super-important in keeping our digestive systems happy. A fiber-rich diet helps our gut microbiota (see page 250) to flourish and helps to bulk up our feces (that's right, readers, I'm talking about poo, but it's important!), meaning we can get rid of waste efficiently. Both of these things equal a happy gut—double pleasure!

WHAT FIBER IS

Fiber is classed as a carbohydrate, and is found in plant-based foods. We consume two different types, both of which are equally important and play a vital role:

× **Viscous or insoluble fiber**—largely found in whole-grain and whole-wheat foods, as well as popcorn, potato skins, dried fruit, nuts, beans, sweetcorn, broccoli, and carrots. We can't digest this, but our gut microbiota can, and its important function is to help other food and waste pass through the gut, keeping our insides happy. Upping insoluble fiber intake can help to relieve constipation

× **Non-viscous or soluble fiber**—found in foods such as amazing oats, barley, pulses, beans, sweet potatoes, peas, apples, oranges, and avocados. We can't digest this but our gut microbiota can, which keeps them happy—it slows our digestion and can help lower blood cholesterol

HOW MUCH FIBER WE NEED

AGE	DAILY AMOUNT
Adults and children aged 16 and over	30g
Children aged 11 to 16	25g
Children aged 5 to 11	20g

To help that start to make sense, I've included fiber in the nutrition box on each recipe page so you can begin to get an idea of how much you get from different meals. For example, just one bowl of Navajo soup (see page 220) gives you almost your entire daily amount at 25.5g!

The key to upping your intake is to embrace in one bowlful fiber-rich ingredients, such as veg, fruit, and whole grains, in your diet.

THE HEALTH BENEFITS

If we don't get enough fiber, our digestive system will slow down and we can become bloated and lethargic, affecting our ability to perform everyday tasks, so it's really important to make sure we are getting enough. Fiber also helps us to feel fuller for longer, preventing overeating and playing a role in weight control.

Eating plenty of fiber-rich foods has been shown to help lower our risk of heart disease—by keeping our cholesterol levels in check—along with type-2 diabetes and some cancers. There is also strong evidence that eating oats or barley with beta-glucans lowers cholesterol. So come on, guys, it's a win win, right?

FOODS THAT CONTAIN FIBER

Following the balanced plate philosophy, starchy carbohydrates should make up about 40% of our meals. Simply switching from refined carbs to whole-grain or whole-wheat varieties can significantly increase our intake of fiber. For example, just switching from a slice of white bread to a slice of brown can quadruple the amount of fiber we get (from 0.5–1g to 3–4g). Other easy switches can be swapping white pasta for whole-wheat, and choosing high-fiber ingredients such as oats, quinoa, beans, pulses, chia, and flaxseeds. When you're shopping, there's one easy tip to remember when it comes to choosing fiber-rich carbohydrates—you want to see the word "whole" in front of starchy carbs in the ingredients list. Don't get confused with "multigrains"—this means there are different grains within the product, but doesn't guarantee that they are whole grains. And of course, eat lots of veggies and fruit, which should make up another 40% of your plate.

Easy wins across the day

Breakfast—choose oats or whole-wheat cereal. Add fruit or dried fruit, nuts, and seeds for natural sweetness and crunch

Lunch—choose whole-grain and whole-wheat options for bread and pasta. Bulk up salads and soups with beans, lentils, plus extra veg and fruit

Dinner—try to always have a simple bowl of salad on the table pre-dinner for hungry mouths to snack on—this is especially useful in encouraging children to build good habits (see pages 264–7). Add extra veg on the side with meals, or bulk up the veg within your meals. If using potatoes, leave the skins on for an added boost of fiber and increased nutritional benefit

Snacks—choose fruit as a snack, whether you're eating it whole or using it in a homemade popsicle (see page 240). A small handful of dried fruit, nuts, and seeds (up to 1 oz), a handful of popcorn, or some veg crudités are also great fiber-rich options

If you feel inspired to up your fiber intake, the best thing you can do is to take a gradual approach. If you suddenly and dramatically increase your intake, you might experience abdominal pain, bloating, and a little wind (which I'm sure we all want to avoid if we can!). Working incrementally will reduce any potential side effects. Also make sure you are drinking enough water (see page 258), as fiber is known to suck up lots of water, helping soften our poo for easy transit.

Strong bones
ESSENTIAL FOR A LONG, ACTIVE LIFE

Our bones are the supporting system of our bodies, and I want you to aspire to having strong, dense bones. If you look at a cross-section of a bone, I think it looks like a coral reef, and just like coral, bones are living organisms that are constantly being broken down and rebuilt. That's why it's so important to understand how they work, and how we can keep them strong, dense, and healthy. The best way to do this is through a balanced diet rich in nutrients, especially calcium, protein, and vitamins D and K, and by being physically active. Crucially, it's never too late to try to improve our bone health.

OUR BONES ARE LIKE A BANK

Up to our mid-thirties, our bones are rapidly forming and being broken down, which is known as our peak bone mass. Once we get into our forties, our bones are broken down faster than they're created. It's really important both as children and as adults to eat a varied and balanced diet in order to build, then to maintain, strong bones. If you can eat and move to guarantee optimal bone health, you'll reap the rewards through every stage of your life, especially in your later years when it really matters. Think about it—what's the clichéd image of an old person . . . a hunched-over, stooping person with a stick. Osteoporosis—cracked, fractured, brittle, or broken bones—can often be the catalyst that sends older people into a spiral of ill health, so I hope that the words on this page will inspire you to take good care of your bone health. I want to see all of you dancing around the table at 90, just like the amazing characters I've met around the world in the areas where people live the longest.

UP YOUR CALCIUM INTAKE

The mineral calcium is integral to the structure of our bones—99% of our calcium stores are found in our bones and teeth! We want those stores to stay there, keeping us as strong as possible, so we need to include calcium-rich foods in our diet (milk, cheese, yogurt, sardines, tofu, broccoli, and ingredients fortified with calcium, such as almond milk). If we don't get enough calcium, our bodies will start to utilize our bone stores instead, which we definitely want to avoid. We need calcium to perform vital functions, including the regulation of our heart's rhythm, blood neutralization, clotting, and the transmission of nerve impulses.

THE IMPORTANCE OF VITAMIN D

Vitamin D helps us absorb calcium from the food we eat, and helps us maintain a healthy bone structure. It plays a role in muscle function, helping us balance and decreasing the risk of a fall, and in turn broken bones, which is particularly important for older people.

We get the majority of our vitamin D from sunlight, when our skin is exposed to ultraviolet B rays. In the spring and summer months, exposing 10–20% of our body (arms, hands, face, and neck) to the sun for about 10–15 minutes a day, being careful not to let our skin burn, can produce enough stores for the winter. The best way to tell whether you're in the right sunlight to make vitamin D is if your shadow is shorter than your height. I also wanted to know whether you could go completely naked to maximize absorption—I think you can; just make sure you find a private place . . . During the winter months, the reduced angle of the sun means we're unable to make vitamin D from sunlight, so we need to top up from food. It's found in oily fish (such as salmon, trout, and mackerel), liver, eggs, wild mushrooms, and in products specifically fortified with vitamin D, such as milk and yogurt. Supplements can be helpful during the winter months.

THE ROLE OF VITAMIN K

Vitamin K—found particularly in leafy green veg like broccoli, cabbage, kale, and spinach—is essential for a healthy bone structure. Some studies have shown an increased risk of bone fractures in elderly people with low levels of vitamin K, so be proactive and try to up your intake. The average adult should be getting 75 micrograms per day—eating just ⅓ oz of curly kale gives us our entire daily requirement in one sitting!

VEG, FRUIT, & PROTEIN

One really common problem when it comes to bone health is that because many of us don't hit our 5 a day target for veg and fruit consumption we don't get enough potassium, which tips our blood acid levels

off balance. If we also don't have enough calcium in our diets, our bones have to release calcium into our bloodstream to neutralize these levels. Getting plenty of potassium from veg and fruit will keep our blood acid levels in check in the first place, which by default protects our calcium stores. This helps to maintain our peak bone mass and reduce age-related bone loss, which in the long run protects our skeleton. Too much salt can also tip our blood acid levels off balance, so keep that in check. Protein makes up roughly 50% of our bone volume, and our bone protein matrix is constantly being remodeled. Therefore, it's important to eat protein regularly, but we need to pair it with veg and fruit to help to balance its acidity.

PHYSICAL ACTIVITY & BONE HEALTH

Regular physical exercise is strongly associated with building and maintaining bone mass and muscle strength. When we're physically active, hormonal change kicks in within our bodies, causing our bones to get thicker and stronger. Basically they're reacting to the environment and what we need at that moment in time, so regular movement and physical activity is a really positive thing. There are two types of exercise we should do for maximum benefit—weight bearing and muscle strengthening. Weight-bearing exercises, such as running, hiking, dancing, tennis, yoga, Pilates, and climbing stairs, help to maintain and build strong bones. Muscle-strengthening exercises, such as using weight machines and elastic exercise bands or lifting kettle bells, help us with balance and coordination, which can prevent us from falling and in turn reduce the risk of fracturing or breaking a bone. For more info on bone health, visit **nos.org.uk** or **nof.org**.

Wonderful water
THE IMPORTANCE OF GOOD HYDRATION

What's the message we should take from this page? Simple—drink more water! Alarmingly, in the UK 60% of people drink just one glass or less a day and we need more. So do it now, get up, go to the tap, pour yourself a glass, and get drinking. Culturally, I think we still have a long way to go before carrying water with us everywhere becomes the norm, but having it around really does encourage consumption. Having water freely available at home, at school, and in the workplace is half the battle won, so if you don't have that, fight for it! Being properly hydrated is essential to life, and if you're trying to be that little bit sharper, then proper hydration could be your best friend.

Celebrating tap water

Here in the UK, we're extremely lucky to have such amazing-quality, free-flowing tap water. We should be really proud of that, and utilize it every day. Mineral water is about convenience and personal taste. Some bottles may contain more minerals than tap water, but the amounts are negligible and we already get these minerals in plentiful supply from our food—it's not reason enough to trade up and there are no health claims that can be made about mineral water. Remember, our tap water is highly monitored before it gets to us, so we can be confident it's completely safe, and we are not losing out by choosing tap. Water filters can certainly be helpful to purify our source further or remove some chlorine, but if you pour water into a pitcher and leave it for 30 minutes, the smell—and hence the taste—of chlorine will disperse.

THE ROLE OF WATER IN THE BODY

On average, our bodies are 50–60% water. One-third of the water in our bodies is found in our blood and between cells (extracellular fluid), whereas the other two-thirds is found within our cells (intercellular fluid).

Wherever it's found, water is a key component of various bodily fluids and functions:

× Nutrient transportation—carrying vitamins, minerals, and glucose between our cells

× Toxin and waste exportation—through regular bowel movements, and urine production via our kidneys

× Synovial fluid—providing cushioning between our joints

× Saliva—helping us to swallow food

× Sweat—helping to regulate our body temperature

× Breath—where we lose water through vapor during the natural process of breathing

WATER INTAKE & OUTPUT

Our water balance is maintained through the fluid we ingest and the fluid we lose through normal bodily functions (see left). The majority is lost through urine via our kidneys, so they're vital in maintaining our water balance. When we don't have enough, our kidneys send a message to our brain that we're dehydrated, and we feel thirsty. There's actually a lag in this message, so if we feel thirsty, we've probably been dehydrated for at least an hour. Kids are even worse at recognizing thirst, so they need to be reminded to drink water often.

HOW MUCH WATER WE NEED

The amount we need is affected by everything from age, build, lifestyle, and activity levels to the humidity around us. Drinks should make up 70–80% of our water intake, with just 20–30% coming from food with a high-water content, such as veggies and fruit.

The European Food Safety Authority guidelines state:

AGE/GENDER	FLUID AMOUNT	TOP UP LEVEL FROM FOOD
Female aged 14 years and over	1.5 liters per day	500ml
Male aged 14 years and over	2 liters per day	500ml
Girls aged 9 to 13 years	1.3 to 1.5 liters per day	400 to 600ml
Boys aged 9 to 13 years	1.5 to 1.7 liters per day	400 to 600ml
Children aged 4 to 8 years	1.1 to 1.3 liters per day	300 to 500ml

Energy requirements are higher for women who are pregnant or breastfeeding, so up your fluid intake, too.

HOW TO STAY HYDRATED

The clue is in the title of this page—good old H_2O is always going to be our best bet, and should make up the majority of our fluid intake. Milk and sugar-free drinks, including teas and herbal teas, coffee (in moderation, of course), and fruit juice contribute too, as do foods with a high water content. Stick to a maximum of one 150ml serving of unsweetened fruit juice per day—this will count as one portion of our 5-a-day, but also means we're not overdoing it on the sugar front.

Try to drink fluids at regular intervals throughout the day to ensure you meet your body's requirements. Water is the best ally to have at mealtimes, because it's neutral, so it won't fight with the flavors of your food.

Staying hydrated during exercise and sporting activity is super-important. The amount of fluid we need depends on the humidity and temperature of the environment, the level we're sweating, and the intensity and duration of the activity. During moderate activity, sip water at regular intervals. With more intensive workouts of more than 1 hour, 50/50 fruit juice/water can help maintain energy levels.

AVOIDING DEHYDRATION

Being even slightly dehydrated can result in us feeling tired, getting a headache, and underperforming both mentally and physically. More extreme dehydration can lead to constipation and kidney stones.

Our urine is the best indicator—if we're properly hydrated it should be either a pale yellow or a straw color. The more dehydrated we get, the darker the urine, so the easiest thing to do is to keep an eye on it.

Sugar—busting the myths
SOME HANDY THINGS TO KNOW

- -

Sugar is a big topic right now. Looking at the effects that eating too much sugar can have on our health throws up big, scary figures, but with just a little know-how, we can all take some simple steps to reduce our intake. Even the British government is on board, having announced a sugary drinks tax to come into play in 2018, forcing industry to reformulate faster—the food revolution has begun!

IS ALL SUGAR EQUAL?

In short, no. Naturally occurring sugars are totally fine, and we shouldn't worry about them, but free sugars are a problem. So what's the difference?

× **Naturally occurring sugars**—found naturally in veg and fruit (fresh, frozen, dried) and dairy products (milk, plain yogurt, cheese), these foods also contain other nutrients, so their health benefits outweigh any negative impact from their sugar content

× **Free sugars**—this refers to sugars added to food and drink, either by us or by manufacturers, as well as sugars found naturally in honey, syrups, fruit juices, and fruit juice concentrates

Free sugars are mostly found in processed and manufactured foods (such as prepackaged meals, cookies, and condiments), and this is what we need to cut down on. Of course, free sugars can be helpful in small amounts to add sweetness when cooking, but portion control is absolutely crucial and using these sugars does count towards your daily sugar intake (see page right). The choices here can be more useful than regular sugar, as they may also give us a little nutritional benefit:

× **Unsweetened fruit juice**—we get vitamin C from most juices, boosting our immune system, as well as the mineral potassium, which our muscles need to function properly. Try to limit consumption to ⅔ cup a day (which counts as one portion of our 5-a-day)

× **Blackstrap molasses**—although not as sweet as other refined sugars, blackstrap molasses is a source of iron, which helps to prevent us from getting tired and keeps our immune systems healthy, as well as providing the minerals potassium, calcium, magnesium, and copper

× **Maple syrup**—made from maple tree sap, it's high in manganese, helping to protect our cells from damage, keeping our bones strong and our energy levels high. It's also a source of riboflavin, helping to keep our eyes, skin, and red blood cells healthy

× **Honey**—produced from bee pollen and nectar, honey is lower in calories than regular sugar, and sweeter, so you can use less. It's also a source of manganese. Manuka honey is thought to contain some antiseptic qualities, and aid in healing wounds

HOW MUCH SUGAR SHOULD I EAT?

In the UK, the current recommended intake per adult is a maximum of 90g of "total sugars" a day—this is a combination of free and naturally occurring sugars. Guidelines for free sugars are very specific (aim for less!):

AGE	MAXIMUM FREE SUGARS PER DAY
Adults and children aged 11 and over	30g or roughly 7 teaspoons
Children aged 7 to 10	24g or roughly 6 teaspoons
Children aged 4 to 6	19g or roughly 5 teaspoons

WHAT SUGAR IS IN MY FOOD?

× Free sugars aren't always labeled as sugar, so can be tricky to spot. Keep an eye out for the following commonly used ingredients, which are all sugars: agave nectar, corn sweetener, dextrose, honey, corn syrup, sucrose, fructose, glucose, and molasses

× Food labels list ingredients in descending order, so in general, the higher sugars appear in the list, the more that product contains

× For extra clarity, use the nutritional information panel on the back or side of the package to find out the sugar content. But remember, this figure doesn't distinguish between free and naturally occurring sugars, so also check the ingredients list to get a feel for what type of sugars are actually in the product

× In the UK, many food and drink manufacturers now use traffic light labeling on the front of their packs, signposting key nutrient values—including sugars, saturated fat, and salt—as green, amber, or red (low, medium, or high). As a general rule, aim to choose food and drinks that would be mainly green and amber across all values—that is, with no more than 15g of sugar, 5g of saturated fat, and 1.5g of salt

TOP TIPS TO REDUCE SUGAR INTAKE

× Choose water instead of fizzy sugar-sweetened drinks to keep you hydrated (see page 258)

× A simple one—don't keep sugary drinks in the house. If they're not there, you can't drink them!

× Make your own breakfast rather than choosing a sugar-laden cereal—check out pages 10–41

× It's easy to confuse hunger with thirst, so try having a glass of water or a cup of tea, coffee, or milk before reaching for a high-sugar or high-fat snack

× Save indulgent, high-sugar desserts for the weekend and special occasions

× Get your kids eating simple savory, veg-based snacks, so their taste buds aren't trained to only want sweet stuff. Somehow my wife has managed to get our younger ones thinking frozen peas are a treat!

The key thing to remember is that eating healthily is about balance. Indulgent foods, such as those high in fats or sugars, can be enjoyed and savored occasionally, just not every day. The majority of our diet should be made up of balanced, nutritious everyday foods.

Cooking with kids
HOW TO GET THEM INVOLVED

I wholeheartedly believe that cooking is up there as one of the most valuable skills you can teach a child, right alongside reading and writing. It's incredibly important to get your kids excited about food, where it comes from, and how to cook it, from as early an age as possible—a kitchen-savvy kid is going to be a much healthier, happier one in the long run. Here are some great tips to keep in mind:

Start them young

Investing the time when they're young and impressionable is absolutely key. Expose them to the widest variety of nutritious foods you can—the more experience and food knowledge they can gather, the more confident they'll become, meaning they'll be curious and try new things.

+ MAKE THE TIME +

We're all slaves to a busy lifestyle, so make sure you put time aside to cook together—keep simple jobs for weekdays, then spend a bit more time at the weekend cooking something more involved. Batch cooking is a great option, as the kids will love the fact that they've contributed towards meals on other days (this is especially good if you've got any fussy eaters on your hands—see page 266). Getting them to help you whiz up smoothies (see page 20), or batches of porridge mix (see page 12) for their breakfasts, is also a quick and effective way to involve them in simple tasks.

START SMALL & BUILD UP

It's always good to start small, with jobs such as picking herbs, spinning salad leaves dry, mixing and measuring, and giving kids decisions to make to empower them. You can then progress to elements of a recipe, then go on to slightly trickier techniques over time. The more they cook, the better they'll get—my older girls are quite happy to have a go at whole recipes these days, whereas the younger two are excited to help out with random bits and pieces. It's just important to spark that hunger to want to be involved.

Have a hands-on attitude

Get your kids to taste, touch, and smell the ingredients that you're cooking with—the more knowledge you can share with them, the better. Explain that it's OK not to like everything, but that it's always good to give it a try, and definitely lead by example—if you're doing something, the chances are they'll want to give it a go, too.

HAVE FUN & EMBRACE THE MESS

After all, kids will be kids! To give yourself half a chance, start off with an organized kitchen, get the kids aprons, and give them stools to stand on. Teach a few house rules, as well as how to tidy up afterwards—instill those good habits now, or you may end up regretting it!

Keep it simple

Sometimes the simplest recipes are best—it's much better to start with something quick and easy and to keep their attention, than to choose something too complicated so they get bored halfway through and scamper off. Start by picking their favorite dishes, then progress to things that begin to challenge their taste buds and push them out of their comfort zone.

USE REAL EQUIPMENT

I'm a firm believer in getting kids to use real equipment. For example, the best and safest way for a child to learn how to use—and even walk safely with—a knife is by using a real knife. Also, it's empowering and confidence-boosting for them to be trusted with adult equipment—under full supervision, obviously!

Grow stuff

You don't need a big garden to be able to grow stuff—a few herbs or tomatoes growing on a windowsill is enough to spark their interest, and will inspire and help to form positive eating habits that will last a lifetime.

Visit farmers' markets

If you can, regularly take your kids to a farmers' market throughout their childhood. I truly believe that because of the passion of the people working there, their incredible and instinctive knowledge, their respect for produce, and their ability to embrace the seasons, your children will develop an amazing understanding of food. You don't even have to spend any money—just take a look around, ask questions, touch, feel, and soak it all in. It will be one of the most powerful experiences in their food education that you can provide, and it'll be super fun, too.

GET INTO THE GREAT OUTDOORS

Celebrating food outside feels playful and exciting, which can help children to relax. Whether it's having fun picking fruit or pulling up carrots, it doesn't need to be complicated—simply grab a chopping board and a few basic tools and you can knock together a delicious salad from a few simple homegrown ingredients.

Involve them in other ways

Try to involve your kids in the ritual of a family meal. Get them to help set the table, and if it's a special occasion, to make name tags or decorations—that way they're already invested in the meal. Get them to pimp pitchers of water with squeezes of citrus, berries, or picked herbs and fill everyone's glass before the meal starts (for more info on hydration, see page 258).

Fussy eaters
TIPS, TRICKS, & HACKS TO HELP YOU OUT

First up, let me say that all the tactics on this page will work on fussy adults just as well as they'll work on fussy children. People focus on how difficult it can be to get kids eating right, but it can be easy, too. Every child is different, and I promise you my mealtimes are far from perfect—it's always total carnage and if we get through dinner without one of them crying, it's a rare victory! Their tastes, personalities, and state of mind are ever changing, and my own belief is that I'm only ever 30 seconds away from anarchy. But, if you stick at it, and use some of these strategies—which I use at home—you will win out in the end. Me and Jools have managed to get our kids to be a pretty well-rounded bunch, who will try to learn to enjoy most things. Ultimately, after that, the rest is down to them.

Don't give up

It's normal for kids to go through phases of liking and disliking things—however frustrating, it's part of growing up. If something's not a hit, perseverance and patience are key. Try 3, 10, 20 times until you succeed. And try not to make a drama out of it. Removing the food without comment is the best way to go. Try again another day. Eventually they'll crack, and if they don't, perhaps they'll never be a fan—and that's OK.

- BE A ROLE MODEL -

Your children will copy and learn from you, so show them the way! Embrace a variety of foods at mealtimes— once they see you eating something, they're far more likely to try it. And if you're really stuck, a cheeky mouthful stolen from your plate, if they're prepared to try something new, is only a good thing.

Reinforce good habits

Try to come up with strategies to spark their interest, and reinforce and encourage positive eating habits over time. It's incredibly important to get kids wanting to eat good stuff on their own, to embrace and be excited by new flavors, textures, and ingredients, to grab their attention and inspire them to step outside their comfort zone and try new things.

— *Set a routine* —

Establish a good routine as early as possible. We try to stick to three meals a day, with a snack mid-morning and mid-afternoon—that way, the kids know where they stand, feel relaxed, and have a chance to build up a hunger. It also gives them a chance to look forward to their meals.

The power of plants

Making it completely normal to chomp on veg and fruit is one of the most powerful things you can instill in any child. Use whatever tricks you can to get them on board. If it takes cutting things up with a crinkle-cut knife, making veggie ribbons with a vegetable peeler, or giving something a funny name to get them to try it, do it! If you can convince them that something is a treat by getting them to try it outside of mealtimes, that can be a smart tactic, too. I find that during that post-bath period when they don't want to go to bed they'll happily try a bit of raw asparagus or a broad bean if it means distracting Daddy from sending them to bed . . . I also always have a bowl of simple salad on the dinner table 10 minutes before I serve up—if they're hungry enough, they'll generally tuck into that while they're waiting.

DISTRACTION OR NO DISTRACTION?

I'm really torn here. I hate toys, TV, and phones at the dinner table. I believe good chat is all you need. Yet, if younger kids are struggling to eat the good stuff, letting them watch their favorite cartoon may distract them long enough to eat up. In reality, I guess a mix of tactics depending on their age is helpful. And ultimately, as they get older, eating, sharing, and conversation is definitely the way to go—and it's good for the soul, too.

Look at the bigger picture

Don't beat yourself up if things don't quite go to plan—look at the whole week and reassure yourself that they've actually done quite well. If you have the odd battle, don't stress about it—we've all been there!

DISGUISING VEGETABLES

I'm not a huge fan of hiding veg, but it works really well! Blitzing or blending them into their favorite dishes is a great place to start—over time you can begin to leave them a bit chunkier, until they eventually stop noticing them. It's more of a stepping stone than a blanket cure.

5 THINGS TO KEEP IN MIND . . .

× Dinner time is often chaos—embrace it!

× Your child is not an adult, so cut them a bit of slack

× If a kid grows it and cooks it, they'll probably eat it

× Focus on what they do like, not on what they don't

× If everyone's eating it, they're more likely to try it

Don't worry, be happy!

If you're concerned about what your kids are eating, the fact that you care already puts you in the Premier League of parenting. My kids can be fussy eaters, and I'm a chef! Have fun with food and try to think long term. Encourage them to do small things over a long period—they'll get there in the end!

Budgeting made easy
MY TOP TIPS FOR CLEVER SHOPPING

Shopping

× Shop around—the best place to buy your veg and fruit might not be the best place to get your meat, fish, or dairy products. It takes more time, but it's definitely worth it

× Shopping online can be a great way to watch what you spend—it's easy to keep an eye on the running total, and to adjust if you've overspent. Plus, the temptations are far less!

× Stock up on staples that have a long shelf life, such as rice, pasta, dried, and canned goods. Often you can buy these things in bulk, and if you've got the storage space, I think it's well worth it. If not, why not see if you can get together with friends or family, bulk buy, then share it out between you?

× Using spices in your cooking adds tons of flavor. Ethnic stores and a lot of supermarkets sell them in big bags—they're a fraction of the price and you get loads more for your money. Simply decant them into airtight jars, label them, and stored correctly they'll last for ages

× Resist buy-one-get-one-free and similar schemes on the stuff you want to limit in your diet—it's only a bargain if you need it!

Menu planning

Menu planning is great, but don't let it restrict you. Flexi-planning is your best option—shop to plan for half the week, then build in meals that are adaptable for the remaining days. This will help you waste less, and means you won't get caught out if your plans change at the last minute.

LOVE YOUR FREEZER

× For recipes, such as Bolognese (see pages 170 and 226), and fish pie (see page 82), double up on ingredients and batch cook so you have lots of leftovers. They make great lunches or last-minute meals from the freezer, and your time-poor self will thank you! Label it up to avoid freezer roulette

× The top drawer of my freezer is full of stuff for adding flavor. Chiles and ginger that are looking a bit sad, ready to grate from frozen, or chopped in advance; curry, bay, and kaffir lime leaves; homemade pestos (see page 232), curry pastes (see page 236), and bags or containers of leftover stock (see page 230). All freeze well and can be used straight from frozen

× Frozen shrimp are often cheaper, are convenient, and are brilliant for super-quick meals, such as my Sri Lankan shrimp curry (see page 50)

- MEAT -

× Visit your butcher—it means you're not dictated by package sizes, and they can help you to shop smart. Always buy the best you can afford

× Eat meat less often, or opt for smaller quantities and bulk up your meals with pulses or seasonal veg—this will save you money, and is good for the planet, too

× Buying a larger piece of meat and making it stretch over multiple meals is a great way to save a bit of cash. I often buy a whole chicken and joint it myself, or cook it whole and use the leftover meat and broth in various ways in the days that follow (see page 230)

- FISH -

× Be open-minded about the fish you choose and talk to your fishmonger—they'll advise you what's in season and what's sustainable, and it'll normally be cheaper

× Look out for sides of fish on offer, and make your own fish fingers (see page 228) for the freezer

- VEG & FRUIT -

× Teach yourself a little bit about seasonality, because when things are in season, they taste better and they're much more nutritious and affordable

× Also stock up on frozen veg—they're great value, available all year, and are nutritious because they've been frozen at their peak—you can just grab a handful of what you need, when you need it

× Frozen fruit is always useful, for breakfast smoothies (see page 20) and popsicles (see page 240)

MAKE YOUR OWN

Making your own pasta (see page 200), pizza bases (see page 94), flatbreads (see page 220), and tacos (see page 86) will save you tons of money, and the bonus is you know exactly what's gone into them, too.

GROW YOUR OWN

Not everyone has a garden, but you don't need one to grow your own food. Lots of plants—herbs, chiles, and many salad leaves—grow happily indoors or in window boxes.

Stock up

A perfectly prepped pantry can be a lifesaver on those days when you need to get something on the table quickly—stock up on all kinds of wonderful things to help you easily inject flavor, such as oils, pickles, vinegars, bouillon cubes, nuts, seeds, dried pasta and noodles, rice, grains and pulses, canned and jarred foods, as well as baking staples. Just remember that condiments are often high in salt, so use with care.

Get lots of herbs and spices in your life—it's a healthy, delicious way to add flavor and can help lower your salt intake. To keep picked herbs fresh for as long as possible, bunch them up, trim the stalks, wrap them in damp paper towel, and pop them into the fridge.

Ingredients round-up
STANDARDS, WELFARE, & GUIDANCE

FOOD STANDARDS

For me, there's no point in eating meat unless the animal was raised well and it was at optimal health. Choosing grass-fed animals where possible, which are free to roam and haven't lived in a stressful environment, is essential—it makes total sense to me that what we put into our bodies should have lived a good life, to in turn give us goodness. It's about quality over quantity, so please choose organic, free-range, or higher-welfare meat and responsibly sourced fish whenever you can.

With eggs, always go free-range or organic, and do the same for anything containing egg, such as noodles and pasta. And please choose organic stock, too.

DAIRY

With staple dairy products, like milk, yogurt, and butter, I honestly couldn't endorse more the trade-up to organic. It is slightly more expensive, but every time you buy organic you vote for a better food system.

ALCOHOL

Some of the recipes in this book use alcohol for added flavor. Although the majority of the alcohol is cooked away, traces may remain, but not in the quantity that would be harmful to a child. If you're cooking for a child under the age of two, leave the alcohol out, or replace it with reduced-sodium stock or unsweetened fruit juice.

FREEZING

Let food cool before freezing, and break it down into portions so it cools quicker and you can get it into the freezer within 2 hours of cooking. Make sure everything is well wrapped, meat and fish especially, and labeled up for future reference. Thaw in the fridge before use. Generally, if you've frozen cooked food, don't freeze it again after you've reheated it.

SALT

We need a small amount of salt so our body can carry out a number of essential functions. Salt helps maintain the fluid in our cells and is used to transmit information within our nerves and muscles. Too much salt, however, can be dangerous—it can raise blood pressure, in turn increasing the risk of stroke and heart disease. A salty diet is especially dangerous for children because their kidneys are not developed enough to cope with it. Generally, try to choose products with less than 0.3g of salt per 100g.

AGE	MAXIMUM DAILY INTAKE
Adults and children aged 11 and over	6g
Children aged 7 to 10	5g
Children aged 4 to 6	3g

Equipment chat

If you want to save yourself a lot of time and hassle, there are a few kitchen kit items and gadgets that I swear by, which will definitely make your life a whole lot easier. A food processor is going to save you hours of chopping and grating every week, and a blender will help you whiz up all kinds of wonderful things in a matter of seconds (see Kitchen Hacks for inspiration, pages 222–41). Vegetable peelers, box graters, and crinkle-cut knives are a fantastic way to add interesting texture to salads, and a pestle and mortar is brilliant for smashing and grinding ingredients to extract maximum flavor. On top of that, a grill pan, some sturdy roasting pans, a set of decent non-stick pans, and some good-quality knives will stand you in good stead. Keep your kit in good nick, your kitchen super-organized, and you'll be well prepped to knock out super-tasty meals the whole family will love.

– A NOTE FROM JAMIE'S NUTRITION TEAM –

The job of our team is to make sure that Jamie can be super-creative with his recipe writing, while also ensuring that all recipes meet the set guidelines. Every book has a different brief, and Jamie's aim with *Super Food Family Classics* is to provide you with lots of tasty, balanced meal ideas you can cook every day, which just happen to be healthy and that fit within a daily structure of calories (see page 244—this is based on a woman's daily recommended intake of about 2000 calories). Remember that these figures are just a guide, and what you eat will always need to be considered in relation to factors such as age, gender, build, and physical activity levels. In order for you to be able to make informed choices, we've published the nutritional content for each recipe on the recipe page itself, giving you a really easy access point to understand what you're eating, should you wish to do so. Remember that a good, balanced diet and regular exercise are the keys to a healthier lifestyle. For more information about our guidelines and how we analyze recipes, please visit: **jamieoliver.com/nutrition**.

Laura Matthews—Head of Nutrition, RNutr (food)

Hungry for more?

For handy nutrition advice, as well as videos, features, hints, tricks, and tips on all sorts of different subjects, and loads of brilliant, tasty recipes, plus much more, check out **jamieoliver.com** and **youtube.com/jamieoliver**.

THANK YOU

You know who you are and how

much I appreciate all that you do

First and foremost, during the creation of this book I've had the privilege of meeting some wonderful people with amazing knowledge when it comes to health, well-being, and nutrition. Huge gratitude to: Kinvara Carey, General Manager at the Natural Hydration Council, Dr Helen Crawley, Registered Public Health Nutritionist, who manages the charity First Steps Nutrition Trust; Dr Emma Derbyshire, Registered Public Health Nutritionist, who founded Nutritional Insight Limited and is an award-winning health writer; Professor Marion M. Hetherington, Professor of Biopsychology at the University of Leeds, with interests in human appetite across the lifespan; Dr Jonathan D. Johnston, Reader in Chronobiology and Integrative Physiology PGR Director, School of Biosciences and Medicine at the University of Surrey; Professor Susan Lanham-New, Professor of Nutrition at the University of Surrey, and a scientific advisor to the National Osteoporosis Society, the UK's leading osteoporosis and bone health charity; Professor Julie Lovegrove, Professor of Human Nutrition and Registered Nutritionist at the University of Reading, with interest in the nutritional influences of cardiovascular health and the development of metabolic syndrome; Bryan McCluskey, Group Operations Director at the Highland Spring Group; Dr Denise Robertson, Senior Lecturer in Nutritional Physiology at the University of Surrey, who looks at how different forms of carbohydrates affect our gut and overall health; Jamie Sawyer, my brilliant personal trainer.

I'm super-lucky to be surrounded by a lot of incredible people, both within my own company and within those companies I regularly work with. All of you contribute so much to the creation of my books, and to the life they go on to have after they're published, both in the UK and around the globe. I can't thank you all enough for the support you give me. It's impossible to list each and every one of you here, so I'm going to keep it short and sweet, but you all know who you are, and how exceptionally grateful I am.

Special thanks must go to the people closest to me, especially those who've been by my side in the physical creation of this book. Firstly, my amazing food team, divine Ginny Rolfe, my Scottish brother Pete Begg, Bobby Sebire, Abigail Fawcett, Georgina Hayden, Christina Mackenzie, Phillippa Spence, Jodene Jordan, Maddie Rix, Elspeth Meston, Rachel Young, Jonny Lake, Francesa Paling, as well as Becca Sulocki. Also, to Claire Postans, Joanne Lord, Athina Andrelos, Laura James, Ella Miller, Helen Martin, and Daniel Nowland. To my talented nutritionists, Rozzie Batchelar and Eretia O'Kennedy, who's covering Laura Matthews brilliantly. Thanks as always to my words girls, my illustrious editor Rebecca Verity and Bethan O'Connor, and to Laura Jones. And of course, huge thanks to everyone else in the business who has played a part— you lovely lot—from marketing and PR to my personal, legal, finance, and IT teams, and especially all you super-enthusiastic office testers.

Big love, respect, and gratitude to Tom Weldon, Louise Moore, and their wonderful teams at Penguin Random House—from art, production, and Ed2, to rights, publicity, comms, brand, and sales, I'm so appreciative of all that you do. Special mention to John Hamilton, Juliette Butler, Nick Lowndes, Bek Sunley, and, of course, Annie Lee.

Big shout out to James Verity, my designer and camera assistant, and the guys at creative agency Superfantastic. Thank you to dude Paul Stuart, and Bradley Barnes, for the epic portraiture. And to Lima O'Donnell and Julia Bell.

To Jay Hunt and the gang at Channel 4, as well as the fantastic team at Fresh One Productions and the crew, led into the fray by Zoe Collins, Katie Millard, and Nicola Pointer, for supporting this book with an awesome TV show, which I know everyone is going to love.

And last but not least, I must thank my brilliant, beautiful family for your love, support, and inspiration. Massive love.

INDEX

Recipes marked V are suitable for vegetarians

HEALTH & HAPPINESS

For a quick reference list of all the dairy-free and gluten-free recipes in this book, please visit:

jamieoliver.com/ super-food-family-classics/reference

SUPER FOOD FAMILY CLASSICS.

Copyright © 2016 by Jamie Oliver. All rights reserved.

No part of this book may be used or reproduced in any manner whatsoever without the prior written permission of the publisher, except in the case of brief quotations embedded in critical articles and reviews.

For information address HarperCollins Publishers Ltd, 2 Bloor Street East, 20th floor, Toronto, Ontario, Canada M4W 1A8.

HarperCollins books may be purchased for educational, business, or sales promotional use through our Special Markets Department.

First Canadian edition

Recipe photography copyright © Jamie Oliver Enterprises Limited, 2016

Jacket and studio photography copyright © Paul Stuart, 2016

Archive photography on page 242 and endpapers © Jamie Oliver Enterprises Limited, 2016
(David Loftus, Jamie Oliver, Jools Oliver, Matt Russell)

Design by Superfantastic

Color reproduction by Altaimage Ltd

Printed in Italy by LEGO

Library and Archives Canada Cataloguing in Publication information is available upon request

ISBN: 978-1-44345-133-8

15 16 17 18 19 IND/LEGO 10 9 8 7 6 5 4 3 2 1

jamieoliver.com

harpercollins.ca